PRESENCE
AND
UNDER HIS
WINGS

Mary Kathy Hicks

JoAnN Hicks
Daughter
In Law

Joe David
(Son)

MARY KATHY HICKS

In His Presence and Under His Wings

Trilogy Christian Publishers A Wholly Owned Subsidiary of Trinity Broadcasting Network

2442 Michelle Drive, Tustin, CA 92780

10 9 8 7 6 5 4 3 2 1

Library of Congress Cataloging-in-Publication Data is available.

ISBN: 979-8-88738-247-0

E-ISBN: 979-8-88738-248-7

In His Presence

"You will show me the path of life; in Your presence is the fullness of joy; at Your right hand are pleasures forevermore." (Psalm 16:11, NKJV)

and

Under His Wings

"He will cover you with His feathers, and under His wings you will find refuge. His faithfulness is body armor and shield." (Psalm 91:4, TLV)

Mary Kathy Hicks

In memory of my mother

Dedicated to

*My mother and to all those who pray as mothers,
grandmothers, and great-grandmothers.*

"Your Presence"

Here within Your Presence, I am free.

There is no other place I would rather be.

Safe within Your arms Your Love I see.

Nothing compares to knowing You're with me.

Table of Contents

Introduction

The writing of this book has a strange origin. Initially, I felt led to write a book, struggling with the Lord because I believe, as I am learning now, that I was scared to open myself up to people not only whom I don't know but also to people whom I do know. This prompting has resulted in one book that is already published, this one, and a few future ones, the Lord willing. I know that I have read books of the great conversion stories of people who have totally turned around from devastative and destructive lifestyles. I have read conversion stories of people who, early on, had a special calling and did great works for the Lord. I sometimes wondered, *What is my story?* And, *Why is it different?* I did meet the Lord early. I knew He saved and loved me. I had so many ups and downs. He still loved me. I made and do still make many mistakes. He still loves me. What does He want me to do, and why am I to write? His love is showing me.

I have seen throughout my life, often the hard way, that it is better to trust and obey than to doubt and ignore the Lord. Proverbs 3:5–6 (NKJV), "Trust in the LORD with all your heart And lean not on your own understanding; In all your ways acknowledge Him, And He shall direct your paths." I am trying to follow this advice, letting the Lord guide me. I do believe He has guided and helped me even during times that I was unaware of it. I can see such times more clearly now. Several times I have told my Sunday school class that one thing I like about being older is that I can now look back to see how the Lord has been there in my life. The reader should realize I speak with no authority as a biblical scholar, but the reader should personally search scriptures and seek the Lord's guidance. These writings are my sharing of what I have seen and do see, like a poem I wrote so many years ago. I understand better now what I wrote and what this poem might mean.

"The Rear View Mirror"

The sparkling eyes, the face of wonder,

Framed by rings of curls,

Through sparkling of youth and innocence,

A wisdom lightly swirls.

I see a reflection as I drive.

How can I help this one survive?

Sweet curls surround a smiling face.

Such joy and hope will time erase?

If the bad in life I could foresee,

Could I direct what this life will be?

There's only one who can with certainty,

The Lord God of all eternity!

Eagerly, each new sight, taste, and smell,

Is carefully cataloged and defined.

Oh, just to capture for a lifetime

Eternal image, hope, and love confined.

I see a reflection as I drive.

How can I help this one survive?

Sweet curls surround a smiling face.

Such joy and hope will time erase?

If the bad in life I could foresee,

Could I direct what this life will be?

There's only one who can with certainty

The Lord God of all eternity!

INTRODUCTION

I will try my best to share some of what I have seen in reflection. Often, I may mix the times when the events occurred with what I saw and felt at the time alongside what I grew to see and even with what I hope to see. I have tried to share scriptures that have helped me and still do. If readers are not familiar with any of these in context, I do hope that they will seek these out for themselves because I know that I may not have served them as completely as I would have liked contextually. I have used the NKJV translations primarily because it is poetic and blends with my use of poems. However, I have shown in some places how different translations can assist and deepen one's understanding of scripture. I have included some of my poems from those written on scraps of paper, napkins, and even backs of bills. I have already provided the reader with two of these poems. I know that I am not a true poet, but I hope these sentiments might strike a chord with others, especially because I wrote them during the period that I am describing. I will use repetition of some thoughts and truths because I needed the reinforcement in my life and because these are critical points. However, much of the revisiting of these will be in the context of new or enhanced understanding. My prayer is that my trust and obedience in this sharing will be helpful to the reader.

A Mother's Prayers

And Hannah prayed and said: "My heart rejoices in the LORD; My horn is exalted in the LORD. I smile at my enemies, Because I rejoice in Your salvation. No one is holy like the LORD, For *there* is none besides You, Nor is *there* any rock."

1 Samuel 2:1–2 (NKJV)

"A Mother's Face"

As a babe, I saw Your love in my mother's face.

Her prayers and loving care drew me to Your saving grace.

And from hers into Your loving arms, I found a place

Where then, in safety, peace, and promise, I could dwell

Where all my fears and dangers You could quickly quell

Where for both my body and soul You say, "All is well."

A peaceful sensation seemed to cover me as I lay, watching something gently blow almost within my reach. I tried to grab it each time that the refreshing breeze blew it closer to me. I could only see it and the colorful things. I could feel something beside me when I grasped, somewhat accidentally, little soft nobs.

The preceding paragraph describes my earliest memory: A memory that has remained with me for more than seventy years, although the colorful things that turned out to be floral wallpaper have faded some in my mind. That sense of peace and overwhelming wrapping of love and comfort I have experienced only one other time in my life. This second experience happened when I had spent a good part of a day talking with the Lord, and then I had a similar sensation minus the curtain and soft nobs and, of course, the wallpaper. I believe an experience like this is being totally in His—the Lord's—presence.

I have experienced closeness many times, just not to that same degree of closeness. I witnessed and felt a similar calm and peacefulness many times within and near my mother. As a young child, I asked my mother about that early memory because I would recall it often, especially then. It was almost as though I was in that moment anew. She told me I was describing a time and place when I was a tiny baby. She had placed me on a bed with a chenille bedspread. Oh, that piece of information explained the little soft nobs! Such bedspreads at that time had raised little tufts. I do wish I had one like that today. I would also enjoy having a chenille robe that would be similar to the bedspread. I am certain I would spend time caressing the fabric. She identified the blowing thing as a thin, nylon curtain. These were popular at that time and would only slightly limit the breeze from the open window.

Such a period I call B.A., "before air conditioning." Having an open window, possibly combined with a fan, offered relief in warm and hot weather. Not only during the day would the open window offer relief from the heat, but the opened window would also provide cooling at night, having only a screen to protect from the outside and bugs. Later, my dad would rig what was called a swamp cooler then. He would use a hose to pour cold well water over what looked like sheets of straw inside the cooler. The room with the window where the swamp cooler was would become cool, almost cold. Dad looked at trees and sometimes used a stick to locate a proper spot, then dug the well himself. He helped several neighbors with this same process.

Those were safer times, so people were not afraid to leave their windows open while they slept, at least, not where we lived. Now we need security systems, locked doors, closed windows, cameras, and many people still worry for their safety. Although I understand the reasons for these precautions, I do try to use prayer for protection as my outer and inner wall of safety. Speaking of walls and thinking about the wallpaper my mother said I described, I realize that I am not a fan of such wallpaper today. Perhaps that is one reason that the wallpaper portion of the memory has faded while the other parts, especially the peace and comfort, remain strong.

One point I have no doubts about in my memories is that my mother always made me feel comforted and that I frequently witnessed what I believe supplied her own source of peace and serenity. She talked to someone and read often out of a book. She prayed and read the Bible. I probably saw this side of mother more than others in the family because I was the youngest by many years and alone with her while others were at school or work. My mother shared that she had worried greatly when she was pregnant with me because she had read that often women who had babies in their later years give birth to mongoloid babies. Although that term is an offensive one today, I understand that it is also an archaic term for Down syndrome. I understand that the discontinued term had something to do with the slanted eyes characteristic. In the 1960s, the term was changed. I know my mother meant no disrespect by using it; we must realize the time she lived. I do wish people today would consider the context of historical circumstances before being judgmental of those from other time periods. I am certain that she meant this syndrome based on both terms and circumstances of her time. Listening to her describe her fears about this possibility, I gathered that she must have spent much time in prayer. Fortunately for me, these prayers helped result in a fairly normal fat little baby with only a little weirdness in personality. I do believe that my mother would have felt blessed no matter what the Lord's answer would have been. I have seen such blessings in both the children with Down syndrome and in the lives of their parents.

I can remember, even when I was still a baby in my crib, seeing and hearing mother praying quietly. My crib was in my parents' room. We had a small house with only one original closet. I slept in my parents' bedroom while the sister closest to my age had the one other bedroom. When I was old enough, I shared a bed with her. My oldest sister was away as she was about eighteen years older than me. My brother slept on a foldout bed at the end of the dining room until Daddy built a den with a large closet and a foldout couch for my brother. Daddy was quite a handyman. As a child, I followed him around, trying to help him lay molds, pour cement, hammer boards, lay bricks, and replace shingles. He, with my help—I say in jest, built a knotty pine den, a lovely front porch, sidewalks, a large, enclosed cooking pit, and even a cement pond for my pet turtles. Other favorite pastimes for him were yard work, gardening, and fishing. I spent time when he was home doing these activities and following my mother around with her chores when he was at work.

As best as I could tell and remember, mother spent much of her day other than doing housework, in praying, and reading her Bible. I believe I would hear her praying not only for her children and for friends but also fervently praying for Daddy. She was rather shy, so I seldom remember her having many conversations with neighbors or friends. I remember a few times that she didn't come to school when I received awards or certificates. I knew that she loved me and was proud of me and that she was a private person. One exception would be conversations with Mom Casey, one of my children's great-grandmothers. They were both dears and, I believe, kindred spirits. The distraction of television did not become available for a few years; however, I did see her spending time in front of the television as she grew older. I remember when Daddy brought home our first television. It was small, few programs were available, and these were in black and white. Now, it seems silly that I would watch the test pattern, waiting for programs to begin. Looking back, I can see how television gradually gained influence on me. It definitely began to distract me from other activities. Some programs were probably positive ones. Some others had negative influences, although I would not realize these until years later. Fortunately for me, there were fewer negative programs then than there are now. Many were neutral in impact. Not as many had what I realize now had negative influences until years later. For example, technology of all sorts can have all three effects. I remember our first telephone—a party line at first. I was sometimes reprimanded for trying to listen to others' conversations. I became very adept at holding down the button under the receiver so that a noise would not signal that someone was listening. Even as a child, I see I was plagued with temptations. We did have a radio. Usually, this was for evening and weekend enjoyment. My most memorable times with the radio were listening to *Inner Sanctum* and *The Shadow*. These experiences were great fun, even though I was a little frightened. Having family around meant that I still felt safe while hearing the scary music and stories.

I guess the absence of modern items made it easier for mother to spend this time in prayer and Bible reading. I have and continue to find that the distractions of the world make it hard to "Be still and know that I am God" (Psalm 46:10, NIV). I was glad that she read the Bible, along with other books to me. Actually, I cannot remember not being able to read. I am sure that there was some point when I learned to read. I could even read much of the Bible (which fact would cause me some problems). I remember even reading *Animal Farm* (my older brother's high school book, I believe). I did not realize the political implications. I just thought those mean old pigs. Reading was an important part of my life. However, most of the books I read were those checked out from the downtown library or ones that my older brother or sister had for school. My first experience learning about evil was reading *Dracula*. I followed mother around as she did housework as I read it because it made me afraid. I remember asking for garlic and a cross. I did receive a little cross necklace, but I learned that the power of protection was not in that little cross. It was Jesus' sacrifice on the cross. My little cross was just a symbol. It would be years before I fully understood more about spiritual warfare, "For we are not fighting against flesh-and-blood enemies, but against evil rulers and authorities of the unseen world, against mighty powers in this dark world and against evil spirits in the heavenly places" (Ephesians 6:12, NLT). It would be even longer before I could embrace the release from fear and full assurance of protection in the Lord:

> Yet in all these things we are more than conquerors through Him who loved us. For I am persuaded that neither death nor life, nor angels nor principalities nor powers, nor things present nor things to come, nor height nor depth, nor any other created thing, shall be able to separate us from the love of God which is in Christ Jesus our Lord.
>
> **Romans 8:37–39 (NKJV)**

The cross provided comfort as a reminder of Christ's great love for me. I still like wearing one to this day. More each day, it brings to remembrance that "For God so loved the world that He gave His only begotten Son, that whoever believes in Him should not perish but have everlasting life" (John 3:16, NKJV). I now understand 1 Corinthians 1:18 (NKJV), "For the message of the cross is foolishness to those who are perishing, but to us who are being saved it is the power of God." I am understanding more about "Whoever desires to come after Me, let him deny himself, and take up his cross, and follow Me" (Mark 8:34, NKJV). Yes, the cross had and has great meaning for me.

Fortunately, many books during that time were uplifting and supported faith. I read *The Robe*, *Dr. Hudson's Secret Journal* (I read all the books by Lloyd C. Douglas), *Ben-Hur* by Lew Wallace, and I read *Quo Vadis* in one day. Reading this last one took me a day, night, and into the next morning. I am not certain if my sobbing at the end of the book was the story or if it was the result of my exhaustion. Along with the example my mother set for me spiritually, she instilled in me a love of reading.

Naturally, I was so eager to begin school, excited because of what I would read and learn. I felt cheated seeing my siblings go to school. Mother would sympathetically indulge me by packing a lunch for me and allowing me to go to sit under a large tree at a neighbor's house. I would read books, write, draw, and eat my lunch, pretending I was at school. I was so disappointed when my first year of school seemed like a disaster. My teacher appeared to be an unhappy person. My most prominent memory of her was that she slapped the hands of certain students with her ruler. Although I never remember having my hands slapped, I would shed tears for the other students. The most unbearable was reading time. The books were so boring. See Spot, see Jane, see Spot run, see Jane run. This boredom resulted in another yielding to temptation. I would carefully rub red crayon on my face and complain. I would be sent to the nurse's office. Once the nurse put the thermometer in my mouth and left the room, I would run hot water over it at the sink. Of course, I would have a temperature. My bag would be sent to me from the classroom, and a call would be made to my mother. I would happily read my own book until mother arrived to take me home. Finally, I was home where I could read something interesting. Mother figured out something was amiss after a couple of these incidents. I confessed to her. She prayed and worked to help me to learn some about what has been a long journey to obedience. This journey continues today.

One stop along the way was clouded with more disobedience and a type of confession. It is strange that I can't remember exactly what I did, but I know it involved going along with what a neighbor girl wanted me to do, even though I knew my mother would not approve. I went home asking my mother to spank me but not to ask what I did. My mother promptly spanked me and never asked anymore. I didn't want her to be disappointed in me. This situation was more impactful on me because I was very aware that I was disobeying. I hadn't even thought about what I was doing wrong other times. As I grew older, I saw how this would affect me in my relationship with the Lord. I am afraid I may have subconsciously thought I needed the Lord to punish me just as I had asked my mother to do. I didn't embrace the loving grace the Lord offered me. Such situations will become evident as I write more. I tried to hide the specifics of what I did because I wanted my mother to be pleased with me; I could not hide things from the Lord.

Although praying and reading were commonplace with mother, I could tell there were times when these activities seemed more intense and fervent. When there was a sickness, a tragedy, or a problem, the tone and intensity increased. However, much of the peace remained even when I had rubeola (we called them red measles). What a painful and terrifying time! My fever must have been exceedingly high. I was placed in a tub of ice. Ever since then, I have hated to be cold. Daddy must have gone to the icehouse

IN HIS PRESENCE **AND UNDER HIS** WINGS

to get so much ice. I loved going downtown with him to the large icehouse. Frequent trips to it were necessary because, for a period of time, we had an icebox and not a refrigerator. Along with times in the icy tub, I was kept in a dark room. My mother would use a cold washcloth on my head. I did sense her care and believed that she was quietly praying. We did not have shots for many of the illnesses that we do today. I remember rubella (we called them German measles—a German physician in 1814 recognized its symptoms first), mumps, and chicken pox. Of course, earaches, colds, flu, sore throats, and other infections were present. My mother and especially my dad had some natural remedies for many of these. I do wish that I knew more about the concoctions that he mixed from things he grew in the garden and flower beds. Doctor visits were rare.

The only other time that I remember mother in what I deemed a more intense prayer demeanor for any of these was during a polio scare. The entire neighborhood seemed on alert. I know that parents were most concerned in the summer. We could not go to many places, especially swimming, or even going out in the afternoon heat. My neighbor and I rigged tin cans connected with a string that we ran across the driveway and through windows so we could talk to each other when we had to stay inside. Rosin was rubbed on the string to make it work better. We did so many things ourselves. We made toy houses and house trailers out of cigar boxes and placed them in the flowerbeds. We created yards and driveways for the houses, using the curbs as the highways for toy cars that would pull the house trailers. Well, back to the fear of polio. I had a stiff neck and some other symptoms that must have concerned mother. She prayed, and I was eventually fine. I have wondered if these were early signs of a disease that I would have years later. Finally, Jonas Salk completed the polio vaccine. We were vaccinated at school. The gun-like devices used were terrifying, and the shot hurt. I do remember this shot and the smallpox shot. I had to have the latter twice because the mark it was supposed to leave did not appear, even the second time.

Mother's fervent prayers were not just for sickness. I remember when we had threats or concerns of a nuclear attack. We had a SAC, or Strategic Air Command, base in my area. I understand these were established during World War II and continued in importance through the Cold War. Evidently, having such a base meant we were a target for a nuclear attack. Because of this concern, my elementary school established drills during which designated parents were instructed to keep supplies in their car trunks and arrive at our school when given a signal. We would then march outside and be placed in various vehicles. We never went beyond this stage of the drills. However, if a real event happened, these cars would drive us via a planned route as far away as possible. I was scared because I would not be with my family. Mother prayed with me, assuring me that all would be fine. The fear of being the target of a nuclear attack would appear again during the Cuban missile crisis. I was in high school by this time. I prayed myself as I believed others were, sitting silently by the open windows at school and wondering if we would be hit by a nuclear attack.

I know mother was praying because she prayed for all her children and my dad. She prayed especially for my brother when he went to college and traveled to Germany as a missionary. All her children, over time, drew close to the Lord and have managed, even through difficulties, to always be under the Lord's protection. I wish I could say I have been the same as my mother. I have seen the power of a mother's prayer in her. I learned to trust in the Lord and to trust in prayer. Although I do not measure up to her, my prayer is that, as a mother, grandmother, and great-grandmother, I might share what I saw and learned with others. Perhaps my greatest regrets center around things I did not do as a mother. I wonder how my mother knew to do some of the things that she did, especially because her own mother died when she was young. Her mother died in childbirth, having my mother's younger brother. Her oldest sister died when the sister was just becoming a young adult.

How did my mother learn? Perhaps, it was as I have—over time and with the help of the Lord. Mother had me much later in life. I had all my children fairly early. Would I have done a better job if I had been more experienced? I do know that I prayed and tried. I am comforted now by the words in Ephesians 5:15–17 (NKJV), "See then that you walk circumspectly, not as fools but as wise, redeeming the time, because the days are evil. Therefore do not be unwise, but understand what the will of the Lord is." I feel that as I grow in the Lord that I am to learn to "redeem the time." I know some translations use "make use of every opportunity." However, I like the sense from the original Greek that "I am to buy up the marketplace." I am now to put everything I have into, in a sense, make up for the lost time. I am "to pray without ceasing" now, investing all I have to "redeem" the time that I didn't invest. I realize that this may be just a special message as I ask for wisdom, learning increasingly about walking in the Spirit and in the Light. I do hope that other mothers, grandmothers, and great-grandmothers, who might feel like me find comfort in reading these thoughts.

The Faith of a Child

But Jesus called them to *Him* and said, "Let the little children come to Me, and do not forbid them; for of such is the kingdom of God"

Luke 18:16 (NKJV)

"Joyful Child"

I run, I play, I jump and dance,
Laughing, knowing with just a glance,
You're keeping me by night and day.
If hurt or afraid, your name I say.
I'm not yet jaded or confused.
I look, learning as one amused.
At night I sweetly say my prayers,
Resting in faith, You've got my cares.

I described earlier how, even as a small child in my crib, I would hear my mother praying. At first, I did not know whom my mother was talking to when she prayed. I just knew that I wanted to talk to that person, too. I began doing so and later learned about the Lord, knowing who He is and why I could talk to Him. In some way, I was blessed because I began with a personal relationship with Him. Rather than beginning with head knowledge that could grow into heart knowledge, I began with the heart. I talked to Him about everything and began with that simple childlike faith that I would struggle to recapture in later life. The first time I remember a quickly answered prayer was when I must have been noticeably young and in church. My feet were dangling from the pew, and the announcements had no meaning for me. Distracted, I saw a spider web underneath the pew in front of me. A bug caught in it struggled to get free. I felt such compassion for that bug. I prayed with simple trust. Later, I looked back to see the bug free and crawling away. I know that this might seem silly to most. However, that was one of my first and most sincere thank you to the Lord. I often think back on that moment and still thank the Lord for granting me such an answer. I hope to recapture such faith and such a soft heart.

Another answered prayer was in response to a nightmare. The original movie, *King Kong*, was re-released in the 1950s. This 1933 version is a laughable version today. To the young child I was, the enormous creature was terrifying. I had dreams that the beast was looking in the windows of my house. In my dreams, I would leap on my trusty tricycle and pedal away, leading him away from my house to save my family and seek escape. Of course, I would not have been able to make such a getaway. For some reason, I didn't tell my family, not even my mother, about these dreams. I had learned from mother to pray. I did, and the dreams vanished. Years later, I remembered the lesson about simple, childlike prayer that I had forgotten. I was teaching preschool Sunday school. I was trying to help them learn Bible verses just as I had as a child. I used a shortened form of the following scripture:

> Don't worry about anything, but in all your prayers, ask God for what you need, always asking him with a thankful heart. And God's peace, which is far beyond human understanding, will keep your hearts and minds safe in union with Christ Jesus.
>
> **Philippians 4:6–7 (GNT)**

I shorten this for them to "don't worry about anything but pray about everything." This was an important lesson I had learned as a child. Through the years, it became praying about important things, then praying about some things or praying about things I can't handle, and finally praying when desperate. As I listened to these sweet children saying this scripture, I wept inside, remembering my childlike faith and knowing I needed to return to it. Thus, began my journey back to praying about everything.

As a child, pets that were sick or injured were subjects of prayer. I had one dog, Brownie, who looked like Tramp from the movie. He was a dear companion. Twice, he came to my rescue. Once, I was walking to the corner store with money in my hand, and the wind caught the bill, blowing it away. He hurried ahead and placed his paw on it, dutifully waiting for me to come to collect it. The second time was when a rabid dog came down our street. Recently, I watched again the movie *To Kill a Mockingbird*. The scene from the movie reminded me a little of my experience, although not the same. My friends ran inside and locked the door, leaving me outside. I was so scared. I worked my way up a pole on their front porch, trying to stay out of reach. Brownie, who was not far away, barked, drawing the dog away. He managed to stay a safe distance from the door and the dog. I saw that I had time to run to my house and called Brownie inside with me. One time Brownie was not able to be the protector. I had pet ducks, Andrew and Martha, and a pet cat. All of them liked to sleep with Brownie, the cat, on top of him. I have always liked the idea of harmony among animals and humans. I would often contemplate the image in scripture "The wolf will live with the lamb, the leopard will lie down with the goat, the calf and the lion and the yearling together; and a child will lead them" (Isaiah 11:6, NIV). My pets gave me hope for this view on earth. Brownie was away with us. When we arrived home, he jumped out of the car, ran into the backyard, and then began angrily chasing the dog next door. We stopped him and discovered my ducks dead in the backyard. Brownie moved them side by side like they always were and nudged them. He evidently knew the dog next door had gotten out of its yard into ours. Brownie, though often acting as the hero, not only looked like Tramp but also had similar habits. He would make his rounds to neighbors' houses. Once, we received a call from a neighbor who found Brownie and saw that he was sick. The neighbor had taken him to the vet immediately. Today a vet might not so readily treat a dog without the owner's being there. My dog had been poisoned. I prayed fervently for Brownie. We had tickets to see the *Ten Commandments* at the movie theater. At the long intermission, I called the vet from a pay

THE FAITH OF A CHILD

phone. I received the news that Brownie would be okay. This is another time I still say thank you to the Lord for His answered prayer and for the neighbor. I remember thinking in child fashion that the neighbor was like the Good Samaritan in the Bible. It seemed like there were many more good neighbors then than now, but I realized that I had better eyes of the heart to see them then. To be accurate, I must attest to the fact that bad neighbors lived nearby then, and good neighbors still exist today.

Regarding pets, I would discover "Good Samaritans" as a teen, young adult, and senior. I had a cat named Snowball. As my lack of originality shows, I am not unique when naming pets. My cat was all white. I came home to discover Snowball was severely injured. I didn't know how it happened. I hurriedly took her to a veterinarian and then an animal hospital. Both told me that there was no hope for her and offered to put her to sleep. With tears streaming, I silently asked the Lord what to do. An employee at the animal hospital seemed to understand my dilemma and gave me an address. I was told that if anyone could save Snowball that this vet could. I hurried to what was a quaint house with a lovely yard. I knocked on the door, holding Snowball in my arms. An elderly Hispanic man appeared. He looked at me and at the cat. "Go around back," he said softly.

He lovingly took Snowball to examine and begin to treat her wounds. He looked at me intensely. "I think I can save her, but you must come every day to spend time with her," he demanded. Filled with hope, I eagerly replied that I would. I did come daily, and Snowball did recover to live a nice long life.

Recently, I learned of such a desire to rescue a cat from one of my grandsons. He was driving when he saw a woman unable to control her large dog who was approaching a kitten. My grandson stopped, but the dog had the kitten in its mouth before he was able to get there. He wrapped the severely injured kitten in a towel and tried vets. Finally, he took it to a shelter where he was told the kindest thing was to put it to sleep to avoid its suffering. Another grandson stopped a person from cruelly throwing a cat in a car trunk. All my children and grandchildren have this same spirit for animals. I know my children loved our pets, beginning with their dog, Pepe, who almost didn't survive puppyhood. One veterinarian worked lovingly to lengthen the life of a sick puppy named Pepe, who would be a dearly loved pet who helped me entertain my children and alert me to problems when they were young. Later, I would have a neighbor help with a dog named Pepper. A wonderful veterinarian helped me through the tragedy of my dear part bobcats, Bob and Buster. One lived fifteen years and the other one sixteen years. Pets are important, especially for children. I spent my childhood with an assortment of pets and playing with neighborhood children.

I remember one neighborhood family that caused disruptions. The parents tended to have noisy parties (I heard my parents refer to these as wild parties). The girl closest in age to me though older might best be described as a bully, although I was not familiar with that term then. She was the neighbor girl I wrote about earlier when I was explaining how I had been disobedient. She had me on the back of her bike riding down the driveway once. Just as she approached her garage, rather than turning, she jumped off, leaving me to crash into the garage, injuring my lip. Another time we were going down a hill in a wagon, and she jumped out, leaving me to overturn at the bottom of the hill, skinning my knees badly. What could have been the most serious incident was when I was looking out the back screen door. Suddenly, I started to close it and heard a noise. The girl's brother had fired what I believe now must have been a bb gun. There was a hole in the screen door at about the level of my head. The Lord was looking out for me as I must have stepped back just in time so that the screen caught the bullet instead of me. Mother was terribly upset. I am not sure what all ensued, but I have a strong memory of my mother and his mother standing on either side of my back fence. My shy, sweet mother was calmly but firmly telling his mother, "I might be twenty years older than you, but I can climb this fence and take care of the situation." The other woman, shocked, left. We never had any problems after that though I was not allowed to play with the daughter anymore. I only saw mother like that one other time when she met one of my older sister's dates at the door. She told him that she had found out things about him and that he was not to come around or see her daughter again. As a child, I tried to reconcile these inconsistencies in my mother. I thought about how Jesus drove the moneychangers out of the Temple. This example helped me at that time, leaving all other concerns about it to God. I thought that sometimes, some people could just make us angry. A recent Bible study has provided deeper insight into this episode in the Temple. It seems to me that if Jesus took the time to make a whip, His actions were not sudden but calculated. Of course, Jesus would know what was happening, what He would do, and what would result. I wonder why it took time for me to acknowledge this point. As an adult, I would find myself angry sometimes. Most often, like my mother, it would be when my children or those in my care were being mistreated or endangered. I admit that some of the angry times were simply when I felt mistreated or wronged. In junior high, I would have to pray without speaking aloud. One scripture that I needed almost daily was, "But I say to you, love your enemies, bless those who curse you, do good to those who hate you, and pray for those who spitefully use you and persecute you" (Matthew 5:44, NKJV). Often, this scripture and prayer were needed because of what we sometimes today call "mean girls." I don't know if they were truly mean but wrapped up in themselves and their social importance. One girl who pretended to be a friend would look for occasions to embarrass or minimize others. One day at lunch, when others were complimenting me about the new red suit that I had on, she acted as though she had accidentally spilled milk on my suit. The looks on the faces of others indicated that they knew that it was no accident. I tried extremely hard not to be mad or upset. I would struggle with how "to be angry but not sin" and how "to turn the other cheek." I must be honest that the older I grew, the less I turned to this prayer. Because of this failure, I would find myself making many mistakes and having to learn many lessons the difficult way about anger, offense, forgiveness, and repentance. We do need to grow in understanding of the Lord. As

I write, however, I am sensitive to how reading, hearing, and learning about scripture at an early age can be so important to a child and how, as adults remembering that childlike faith can lead the adult to a deeper yet still childlike faith.

Yes, thanks to my mother and being able to read so early, I was exposed to scripture. Most importantly, I had encouragement to memorize scripture. Programs at church for children had lovely little emblems to pin on your clothing. These pins indicated levels to pass for reciting scriptures. I am not sure why, but I seemed to know that quoting these scriptures in times of trouble would help me. I also seemed to know that I could talk to the Lord or say these scriptures in my mind rather than aloud. In this way, I could access these helps no matter where or when. I had to talk to the Lord in such ways, especially in first grade, because it was a confusing and, often, unpleasant experience. Later, I remember using scripture as I tried out for the relay team. I am not sure why, but I had to try out with a year older group than my age. I would pray earnestly before, during, and after tryouts. "I can do all things through Christ who strengthens me" (Philippians 4:13, NKJV). Years later, I would cling to this verse many times, remembering how it strengthened the faith of that little girl. I made the team as an alternate. I eventually made the competition team because I was faithful at passing the baton and could run the curves better than a child who was faster than I was.

Sometimes my prayers could be heard by others, such as one time walking home from school. Bullies were not only on my block but also in the school. One such boy thought that it would be great fun to lasso me with a rough rope. He drew it tight around my neck. I dropped and thought I was going to be choked to death. I think I yelled, "Help me, Jesus!" Another stronger boy knocked the bully away and set me free. Although I had visible rope burns on my neck, I was otherwise fine. I believe the boy to my rescue was Nelson. He was my heaven-sent hero and would remain a good friend through elementary school. He may have moved because I do not remember him in later years. I believe this incident helped me to see how the Lord uses people to answer prayers.

I think that the Lord used me at least once during those early years, although I was not consciously attempting to do this. This time reminds me of a quote by C. S. Lewis, "God's presence is not the same as the feeling of God's presence, and He may be doing most for us when we think He is doing less." My friend Bethany lived across from the school. I would sometimes be allowed to stop at her house to play. I do know that we spent time together. I cannot remember exactly how, but over time, I shared with her my relationship with the Lord and how I had accepted Him as my Lord and Savior. I had been baptized at my church even though some people in the congregation considered me too young to do so. However, I had no doubts. I remember my baptism vividly and did understand that He came, died, was buried, and rose so that He became the sacrifice for sin. I accepted His free gift of grace. I remember that Bethany became ill. The details of her illness were not clearly shared with the class. I gladly volunteered to take assignments to her on my way home from school. I was so shocked and saddened to learn that my dear friend Bethany had died. It was exceedingly difficult for me. Her parents asked my mother to bring me by shortly after her passing. They shared a note she had written. This note explained that I had helped her learn about Jesus and that she had accepted Him as her Lord and Savior. They told me that because of her faith that they, too, had accepted Him. I did not understand all of this at the time and still think back on it. How natural sharing the Lord with my friend seemed then. Why is it sometimes so difficult now? How wonderful that the Lord can use us for His purpose even when we seem oblivious to it. It has taken many years for me to understand the simplicity, yet depth, of Jesus' words in John 15:5 (TLV), "I am the vine; you are the branches. The one who abides in Me, and I in him, bears much fruit; for apart from Me, you can do nothing." I believe my child's faith found me just abiding in Him, and He let His power flow producing His fruit. I do look forward to seeing Bethany again in Heaven and maybe even Nelson.

I believe a time when I consciously prayed that I would help someone was with my daddy. It seemed that he always had to go to work late Saturday night, working until early the next morning to get the Sunday morning paper ready. He worked at a newspaper. He did not go to church with us. I worried about him. I knew my mother prayed for him and some of the issues he had. I loved spending time with him on projects, fishing, and running errands. He was very athletic. I liked sports, so we spent time watching, listening, and playing different sports. I prayed awfully hard for him. He would sometimes go to church on Sunday evenings and Wednesday nights. He started reading his Bible. He seemed to be a changed person, reading his Bible and studying scripture. I still have a few typed pages of the study he did.

I believed it was my prayers. I learned from my older brother that mother had helped lead him to the Lord and that my daddy had some type of vision or dream letting him know that he needed to make a decision. Later, the Lord would help me to see that we can play a part, but He is the one who, by the drawing of the Holy Spirit, brings others into His fold.

As a child, I sensed and accepted His presence naturally, like breathing. Once I felt a strong urging that I was to go to see my grandmother. We were scheduled to go sometime later. I had to go the next weekend. I guess I made such a fuss that we went. Everything seemed fine. I do remember my grandmother telling me, "I knew you would come." As we arrived home, we learned that my grandmother had passed. Although I was sad, I was not overwhelmed. Somehow, I felt that what she told me meant that she knew that she was going and that she was saying goodbye. Also, I recall how traveling to her funeral and riding in the backseat, I saw beautiful rays of sunlight. I felt peace for her and peace for me. I never told anyone this before. I can't believe I am sharing it with everyone. Standing beside the bedside of my uncle, I would have a similar peace. He was in the hospital and was suffering. It was not a pleasant sight or passing. My mother had trouble staying in there. All I know is that the Lord covered me and kept me in His care. Thinking back, I should have been upset, even traumatized by his death. The only explanation I can give is that it was the presence of the Lord. I trusted Him, and He was there for me.

I would be remiss if I included these precious memories without sharing what happened after my grandmother's funeral when we returned to her house. I didn't understand it at the time because I was so young. Through my experiences, I learned that peace could quickly be shaken by others when they are motivated by greed and selfishness. My father was one of many children. I am not sure, but there may have been eleven or more. The relatives were grabbing and taking things from the house. My father was so upset. I am not sure what all he said or did, but we left quickly. I know we had a table-cloth grandmother had crocheted. I believe we already had it, but I can't be sure. I still have it, although it has a tear in it now. I remember that my father taught me to crochet a little, and perhaps so did grandmother. I can't say that I was ever exceptionally good. The memory of this event is a strong one. Also, I remember that daddy was upset about his family giving grandmother's family Bible to the minister as partial payment for the funeral services. He tried to buy it back from the minister who had sold or hocked it for cash. Daddy tried to find it but never did. Now, I understand more about how inheritance can be good, bad, comforting, or painful in earthly terms. I would grow from seeing my inheritance in Christ as much more than my eventual home in heaven; I had an inheritance to enjoy on earth as well. I started to understand about treasure. My wish is that the treasure could be because the individual values the object because the person who passed valued it and because of the memories of the person who has passed. Certainly, the passing of a loved one can create challenging decisions. I know when both my parents had gone to be with the Lord, dealing with what they had left, which would seem small to most, was all the feelings that I mentioned. Thieves broke into their house taking glass doorknobs, curtains, miscellaneous items, and the bow and arrows my daddy had made. The bow and arrows were what I lamented. Some of the other items caused much work to figure out replacement. Interestingly enough, what sold quickly and for a surprising amount were items from the garage. Daddy loved salvage stores and would buy unusual things, so I observed the purchases as I tagged along as a child. He used empty jars with the lids nailed to a shelf in the garage to organize and store treasures such as nails, nuts, bolts, and other items. What is a treasure to one can be junk to another. What is junk to one can be another's treasure. As I have grown, I have seen in practice lessons from scripture about treasure, inheritance, and value.

I still have many more lessons to learn. I would encourage the reader to search through the Old and New Testaments looking for lessons about treasure and inheritance. If I shared just what I learned, I would need another book. I will share a few scriptures for now:

> The LORD is exalted, for he dwells on high; he will fill Zion with his justice and righteousness. He will be the sure foundation for your times, a rich store of salvation, wisdom, and knowledge; the fear of the LORD is the key to this treasure.

Isaiah 33:5–6 (NIV)

In Matthew 13:44 (TLV), Jesus explains, "The kingdom of heaven is like a treasure hidden in the field, which a man found and hid. And because of his joy, he goes out and sells all that he has and buys that field." In recent years, I have been learning to rethink what treasures are and, in some ways, to return to ideas of childhood treasures. The sunshine dancing on the water and shining on my face, the fragrance and beauty of flow-ers, the appearance of butterflies and birds, the gentle breeze blowing the trees, the laughing and smiling of my children, grandchildren, and great-grandchildren, the peace of a baby sleeping in my arms—all these and many more are precious treasures. Although throughout my life I have seen the beauty of these treasures, I have let earthly items steal time away from what is of true value. I lacked the wisdom and understanding that, sur-prisingly, I seemed to hold to intuitively as a child. The Lord, His presence, His wisdom, His understanding, and His gifts are the most valued. Time with Him is the most precious. Daily now, I read the following to help me to remember these points:

Happy is the man who finds wisdom,

And the man who gains understanding;

For her proceeds are better than the profits of silver,

And her gain than fine gold.

She is more precious than rubies,

And all the things you may desire cannot com-pare with her.

Length of days is in her right hand,

In her left hand riches and honor.

Her ways are ways of pleasantness,

And all her paths are peace.

She is the tree of life to those who take hold of
her,

And happy are all who retain her.

Proverbs 3:13–18 (NKJV)

Now, I often long to stay in the innocence of childlike faith but know that we must grow up or mature in
our faith. Doing so can bring obstacles. I have found that
as I moved further from staying in the Lord's presence,
the more I became confused and looked to my own or
to someone else's wisdom and understanding. A love of
learning has helped me but also hindered me. If the Lord
continues to lead me to author another book in the future, I will explain this complete process and the problems in it. I did have opportunities to learn from those of
faith as well as those of the world. However, I had some
struggles discerning those in relationship with the Lord
from those in religious pursuits.

Discerning Relationship from Religion

Yet indeed I also count all things loss for the excellence of the knowledge of Christ Jesus my Lord, for whom I have suffered the loss of all things, and count them as rubbish, that I may gain Christ and be found in Him, not having my own righteousness, which is from the law, but that which is through faith in Christ, the righteousness which is from God by faith; that I may know Him and the power of His resurrection, and the fellowship of His sufferings, being conformed to His death.

Philippians 3:8–10 (NKJV)

"Right or Wrong"

At the altar, kneel and pray,

Seeking guidance and the way.

All the rules and the guides,

Seem now but clever disguises.

Can right come out of wrong?

Can disharmony bring a song?

Will the night produce the day?

Will the darkness light the way?

Loneliness creates new hope.

Despair teaches me to cope.

As the rules seem broken now,

Jesus, you bring right somehow.

Out of questions, answers rise.

And a loser gains the prize.

Many of my struggles in faith most certainly were completely my own doing; however, ironically, some struggles and doubts were, in part, from religious teachings. Secular and academic training did create some problems, although faulty truths somehow seemed easier to spot in these than in some of the religious ones. I am today so grateful that I began with the relationship with the Lord so that when doubts and tossing occurred that I could ask personally and run back to the safety of my relationship with the Lord.

One of the first incidents as a child would be during vacation Bible school. My neighborhood had families who were members of different denominations. We all seemed to get along fine with each other as neighbors, at least with those who did go to church. In my child's mind, I thought that if we all worshiped the Lord, then we should all be comfortable reading the Bible, talking about Him, and asking questions. During the summer, almost all denominations had a Bible school. These schools were scheduled for different weeks so that children would go to one another's events. I know that I went to three different denominations' schools. I said in an earlier chapter that being able to read the Bible early would cause me a problem. Well, at one denomination's Bible school, I began to ask questions about what the teacher was saying as I was reading the scripture myself. I sincerely thought I was helping. After the third episode, I learned that I had been asked not to return. Evidently, my questions caused issues because they must have centered on the doctrine that differentiated denominations. As a child, I learned to keep my questions to myself and to notice for the first time that those who believed in the Lord had major differences of opinion.

Another time was when I delivered the sermon for youth Sunday. The members were kind and understanding. However, I sensed that they considered it youthful ignorance when I said that I saw indications of a lack of love for all people within the church. I felt what I saw was true. I must admit I was and always have been not really a denominational person. Because of my beginnings, I was focusing on my relationship with the Lord and not the religion. I had experiences with various denominations in situations other than Bible school. Sometimes I would go to church with a neighbor whose son was in my class at school. I described my memories of the prayer services at this church in an earlier book that I wrote. The mother of this boy owned a millinery shop. I loved her shop, where I learned to make hats. I began making doll clothes by hand in second grade so that I could have beautiful items for my Betsy Wetsy doll. Having limited income, making these clothes myself meant my doll was not lacking in fashion. As a teen, I would make little formals and tuxedos for Ken and Barbie dolls for prom decorations. These doll clothes were made by hand. I even began making some of my clothes by hand in elementary school. Sitting in front of my daddy sewing inspired him to buy me a used Singer. This launched my sewing of many of my clothes, even coats, formals, and wedding gowns. I designed hats, thanks to my neighbor's instructions and supplies to go with my special dresses. I even won a Singer Sewing Contest while I was in junior high for a dress I designed and made. In high school, I was selected as a contestant in my city's pageant, which could lead to the Miss America Pageant. I used my sewing abilities to make most of the clothes needed for events and competition. Also, I designed costumes for quick change on the stage. The lights would go down and then come right back up. I would be attired as the next period character I would portray. Isn't it interesting how the Lord provided the skill I would need? I would meet many individuals of different backgrounds and faiths during this period. Although I became friends with a few of the contestants, I discovered this was not the world for me and gained understanding of inner versus outward beauty. The most important outcome of this experience was meeting my wonderful Christian coach and his wife, who would become my friends for life. Unfortunately, I grew lax in later years, spending little time on the inside of garments to save time. Being able to make my own dresses and hats became more important as I grew older.

At some of these bigger churches, people usually wore nice outfits, and the women and teen girls would often wear hats, gloves, and heels to church with these outfits. Although I never felt lacking in my childhood or youth, my family definitely did not have the same amount of money as my girlfriends' families did. However, I was able to equal or sometimes surpass their outfits because I could create my own unique ones. Some girls would be disappointed when others arrived with the same outfits they had on, while mine were always originals. I would realize later that what we wear does not matter in terms of who we are and, especially, to the Lord. I do still like to put on my best for services but for a different reason. I now like to do it to honor the Lord with my best, realizing that my inside needs to be what is honoring him more than the outside. As a young married, I attended a church by the coast. The pastor there actually advertised that people were welcome, even in beach attire. He was one who focused on what was inside that mattered and that the Lord wanted all people to come to Him. The crucial point was to share the Lord's message of love and grace with all that we could. Also, that pastor made an interesting point one day that perhaps rather than being in social gatherings at the church that the Lord might somedays prefer that we stay home, taking care of the needs of our families. Later, I would understand that he probably was saying that we need to do work guided by the Holy Spirit and not by what we thought seemed good. A few times, I have realized that I was doing things that were good and seemed visibly *Christian* but was busy for the wrong heart reasons.

Although I grew spiritually over the years, the process was still confusing while I was in school, but I did find some inspiring times. As friends in the neighborhood and at school, we found ways, most of the time, to deal with individual differences among our different denominations. Issues such as mixed swimming, dancing, and the format of services seemed to fade or blend as we navigated our social gatherings considering denominational concerns. I would pray, read my Bible, and ask for guidance. Honestly, though, I admit that as I entered college and beyond, I found worldly logic confusing, diffusing, and fusing into decisions until mistakes and missteps brought me back to what really works. Eventually,

I had friends from most of the major denominations.

In high school, we had a Youth for Christ Club with those from my high school. We, leaders, represented many different denominations. We met on Friday mornings before school at a church by our high school. I commend that church because we were not affiliated with them. As leaders, we planned the programs, having funny skits, upbeat presentations, and sharing about the Lord. We began to have good crowds of students, both those who attended church and those who didn't. We had a conflict when the high school coach wanted a meeting at the same time as ours. Some of the star players not only attended but also were leaders of our club. A compromise was reached. I loved the fact that the focus was not on a religion or denomination but on the Lord. I know a few, and maybe others, who came to know the Lord from these meetings and who made new associations with those who attended a church and those who did not. I remember one young man who did not seem offensive but was part of what we thought of then as the wrong crowd because of their cars and tendencies to have group rivalries. After one Friday meeting, he talked to me and indicated that he was not certain that he could belong to a group like those of us trying to serve the Lord. I decided to go on a date with him to reassure him that the Lord loves everyone. While we were driving in his car, several cars from his previous group came near, trying to get him to race with them. He stopped and went to talk to them. I heard him tell them that he wanted them to go away but that he would take me home and that he would meet them later. I don't know if he met them or not. He never asked me out again. I know that he did make a profession of faith in the Lord. He did not attend my church but another one. These days it might be less safe to venture as I did. I do know that Jesus did not, while on earth, differentiate among distinct groups. He made it clear that all of us are sinners and that all of us need the salvation that He offers. He "is not willing that any should perish" (2 Peter 3:9, KJV). I wonder if we push away the very people to whom the Lord wants us to give the good news. Diverse groups, different denominations, and different fears do become hindrances to spreading that Jesus came to seek and save the lost (everyone).

As an adult, I have found, as then, that those who truly seek the Lord personally find more commonalities in their faith than differences. In undergraduate studies, one dear friend was a Catholic nun who donned her nun's habits on campus. She was great fun, and we enjoyed each other's company and discussions. I remember some awful male students who tried to shock and upset her by putting a copy of *Playboy* in front of her. She calmly looked at a few pages, closed it, and said, "There's nothing in there I haven't seen before." She had spoiled their sport. I understand that she was among nuns killed serving in Africa. Another great friend of mine was a nun in Paris; we met when I was leading tours there during some summers. We both loved Molière's comedies. Through her visits to cathedrals, I gained a greater understanding of the meanings of the construction of these places of worship. I learned how they were designed to draw people to the majesty and glory of God and to lead them to worship in reverence and awe. I learned that the building taught through glass and stone the messages of God. I wrote a little about a few of these in an earlier book. I must admit that, just as in college, my hanging out with a sister in full habit caused some strange looks and reactions from observers in Paris. Perhaps the funniest was when my friend was helping me to run to catch my train. A train on an adjoining track had soldiers hanging out the windows. I was much younger then. Some of the soldiers would make typical "wolf calls" and then suddenly stop as they saw the nun behind me. She and I laughed many times about this incident. One friend I almost never had was one who was fearful of me because she knew that church I went to and was afraid denominational differences would cause me to disavow her. However, we became good friends. Even as an adult, I see that those who seek the Lord personally and not through "religion" are similar in their views because we are part of His family, with some differences like all siblings but with the same Heavenly Father, Lord Jesus Savior, and Holy Spirit Guide. If we stay in a relationship with the Lord, daily listening to our Guide as we read His word and asking for understanding in prayer, we should be able to worship and serve in peace and love.

Some of the worst decisions I made in my life were the result of a faulty understanding of the scriptures and wrong advice from leaders who I thought were following the Lord's will. I must accept much of the blame myself. I began to spend less time in prayerful reading of scripture and study, talking to the Lord and seeking His wisdom, and I began to listen more to what others had to say and try to filter their views and the world's wisdom. Looking back, I believe that some leaders sincerely thought they were helping as much of the focus shifted to cultural situational teaching and differing doctrinal perspectives with sparse attention to scriptural truths and study. I definitely noticed less emphasis on prayer and little looking for the guidance of the Holy Spirit in teachings. I have heard some pastors today admit that they misunderstood and misspoke in the past, having the Lord show them where they had lacked knowledge, understanding, and wisdom. It is a comfort in some ways to know that I am not the only one who can look back on such lacks. However, I should have held to a scripture that I learned as a child, "Study to show thyself approved unto God, a workman that has nothing to be ashamed of, rightly dividing the word of truth" (2 Timothy 2:15, JUB). I have learned that this advice that Paul gave young Timothy was critical, not only for teachers and pastors but also for Christians. I like this translation because it is close to the version I learned as a child and makes it clear that we must work to understand God's word and the truth that is in it. We need to depend on His guidance, being in His presence, in this earnest work anew each day. A quote by C. S. Lewis says, "Relying on God has to begin all over again every day as if nothing has yet begun." As we rely on Him, we can be led to knowledge and truth. One such truth is that we are one church with the Lord Jesus Christ as our head. I recently heard a pastor say that when the Lord sees us that He sees one church—His. It seems that we often spend so much time trying to divide ourselves rather than seeking daily to get His help in making us function as one body and letting Him teach us. I wonder if part of the problem is the daily process required by the individual. I know we are told, "And do not be conformed to this world, but be transformed by the renewing of your mind, that you may prove what *is* that good and acceptable and perfect will of God" (Romans 12:2, NKJV). If we seek a relationship with the Lord and don't try just to participate in a religion, we should all then be under the same guidance and renewal. I let myself become confused and misled. I also failed to be diligent myself. I wish that I had not drifted from my child's faith, seeking directly the Lord first and asking for His guidance, but I understand that I needed others to help me grow. The Apostle John warned us in 2 John that there would be deceivers. Therefore, there are those who are deceived by them. Then, I might have avoided the bad decisions I made if I had fully understood the things I know today.

Struggles in Faith

But let him ask in faith, with no doubting, for he who doubts is like a wave of the sea driven and tossed by the wind.

James 1:6 (NKJV)

We may ignore, but we can nowhere evade, the presence of God. The world is crowded with him. He walks everywhere incognito. And the incognito is not always hard to penetrate. The real labor is to remember, to attend…in fact, to come awake. Still more, to remain awake.

C. S. Lewis

"Anchored"

In the swells and in the waves
And the surf crashing in the caves
Someone calls the me that longs to be
Pulling me farther out to sea.

Seagulls soaring oh so high
Makes my spirit with them fly.
Sunshine melts the icy me,
Warming, rising from the sea.

A new night, a new day, and surprise
Brings clear emotion up to rise,
Creating a new and different me.
Moonlight rests on the shining sea.

Sifting through the sands
Gently falling from my hands,
Feelings once wild and free
Subside as You rescue who is really me
Anchored by You in the sands of time on
Your peaceful sea!

I mentioned in the last chapter how my struggles and wavering about what I should do often were a result of what I saw and heard in different denominations. Subtle teachings that appear within whichever one of these denominations one finds oneself can be troubling. Even non-denominational churches can lead one amiss, even if unintentionally. However, I have determined over time that the presence of the Lord and personal relationship with Him can result in friendships of faith despite the major difference in doctrinal denominations. I know now how I have been affected by these sometimes minor and sometimes major misguidances. I am so thankful that because my beginnings were with the Person of Jesus Christ and His Presence, I have had an anchor to pull me with either a gentle tug or a strong jerk back to Him. I have experienced evidence of scripture, "This *hope* we have as an anchor of the soul, both sure and steadfast, and which enters the *Presence* behind the veil" (Hebrews 6:19, NKJV).

I began to see early on a shift in churches' teachings from the message of the Lord's love and saving grace to a focus on dos and don'ts. I do believe that it is important to understand the Lord's precepts and know that we need guidance in how to live, relate to others, and regulate our own personal thoughts and actions. In retrospect, I understand better now the reason for adding text in the AMP version of Proverbs 22:6, "Train up a child in the way he should go [teaching him to seek God's wisdom and will for his abilities and talents], Even when he is old, he will not depart from it." This translation adds clarification that is consistent with other ones, such as NIV, NKJV, and NET. How can parents know what the child's way is unless they teach the child to seek God's wisdom and will? Discipline and dos and don'ts can help the child but only work if in the company of teaching the child to connect to and be in a relationship with the Lord. The child must learn to seek, understand, and follow the Lord's guidance. I guess Eli knew this point when He told young Samuel that it must be the Lord speaking to the boy. He didn't say, "Let me come to hear what He is telling you, or let me tell you what the Lord wants." He instructed Samuel to answer the Lord and listen to Him for himself; please, refer to 1 Samuel 3 (NKJV). However, I noticed that often the teachings in churches as I grew from youth to young adulthood focused increasingly on social issues. Evangelism was still present with some of the emphasis on salvation and eternity, but the concept of spiritual growth seemed to focus on legalism—what you should and should not do. I know that I could have avoided many mistakes and troubles if I had learned more of the why behind these precepts. I was often pulled away from my early training to seek the Lord's guidance. I began to feel tossed from one direction and then to the next. Sometimes I found myself drifting with the tides of societal trends. It seemed that the more I strived to live by what I was understanding to be what I thought at the time was acceptable behavior and living, the more I felt myself sinking under swirling failures. Often, when this happened, I thought I was caught in an undertow like the ones my father repeatedly explained to me how to deal with when we would go to the beach when I was young. I understand that today, like many terms from the past, the term undertow is obsolete and that these are rip currents. I know that young children and weak individuals can be at greater peril from these, but even strong individuals who are unaware and don't know what to do can be in danger from strong and especially fast rip currents. Spiritual rip currents can be equally catastrophic for the individual.

I have since learned more about how important it is to grow up in the Lord and continue to learn spiritually. Just as with rip currents, one must be on the lookout for warning signs. The Lord often sent me small warnings and pulled me gently to safety by a variety of means.

Sometimes it was a person, a program, a reading, an insight, an event, or an internal prodding. A dangerous rip current can appear without warning. Dangers spiritually often did appear suddenly in my life. Many times, I was almost carried out and underwater. During these times, I see that the Lord provided lifelines for me. These near disasters range from joyous rescues to painful recoveries. It has and is still taking time for me to learn and, yes, to return to the personal relationship and guidance of the Holy Spirit. I do believe that it is important to seek counsel and to ask leaders for advice. I have learned that it is important that such counselors and leaders be grounded in strong personal, spiritual relationship with the Lord for me to rely on their counsel. Inexperienced and confused sometimes by religion versus relationship foundational basis of these individuals, I made mistakes. Another crucial point I have learned is that accepting counsel and leadership means matching what one hears with scriptural truths and one's own daily asking for the same counsel in a closer and closer walk with the Lord.

I, too, often accepted counsel without the matching process that I described. In my spiritual naivety, I thought that someone's position as an expert in a particular field and that the fact that the person was a professing Christian provided enough proof that I should put my trust in the person's counsel. Two of the worst decisions of my life and ones that would discourage and haunt me were the result of not going directly to the Lord, searching in His word, and waiting for the guidance of the Holy Spirit. When I say, "discourage and haunt me," I mean that I began to see myself as a failure as a follower of Christ. I let further confusion from misguided teachers of the Word confuse me. I would be haunted by thoughts that, like Adam and Eve who sinned that I might be hiding from His presence or, even worse, cast away from His presence—see Genesis 3 and 4. I would hear sermons that seemed to indicate that the Lord was angry with me, would punish me, and turn from me. After one of these bad decisions, I wanted to give up trying because I felt that I had so failed my Lord. It was during these times that I am so glad that I had established a personal relationship with the Lord early on before I would be confused by all the events, counsels, and teachings. I still knew to talk to Him. Somehow, I knew that He loved me no matter what I did. I sensed His presence even if I tried to hide or run from it. I had some of His Word in my heart that would come back to me. I know I surprised even myself once when a well-meaning person knocked on my door, determined to share the gospel and save souls. This person asked me, "If you were to die, would you go to Heaven?" I calmly and immediately answered, "Yes." Frustrated, the person kept trying to rephrase and expand the question. Each time, I was confident with my answer of secured salvation. I am not certain that the person was sufficiently satisfied with my answers, but he departed. Over time, I have come to understand that my early grounding in the relationship with the Lord solidified my anchoring at this point, guarding me. My helmet of salvation defense was in place, even if nothing else was working as it should. I would later learn more about the body armor available to me as described in Ephesians 6:10–18 (NKJV).

> Finally, my brethren, be strong in the Lord and in the power of His might. Put on the whole armor of God that you may be able to stand against the wiles of the devil. For we do not wrestle against flesh and blood, but against principalities, against powers, against the rulers of the darkness of this age, against spiritual hosts of wickedness in the heavenly places. Therefore take up the whole armor of God, that you may be able to withstand in the evil day, and having done all, to stand. Stand therefore, having girded your waist with truth, having put on the breastplate of righteousness, and having shod your feet with the preparation of the gospel of peace; above all,

taking the shield of faith with which you will be able to quench all the fiery darts of the wicked one. And take the helmet of salvation, and the sword of the Spirit, which is the word of God; praying always with all prayer and supplication in the Spirit.

I would struggle for years learning increasingly about these verses and will mention more about when and how I learned as I continue. I was certain about my salvation even when I heard opposing doctrines, read scriptures that I wasn't sure I understood, and questioned my failures. I know when I found out that I had myasthenia gravis, some told me that if I had enough faith, I would be healed. I still have it. However, I never doubted the Lord. In fact, He has healed me at times in many ways. I have learned much from myasthenia gravis and may be healthier today because of it. It has taught me daily, even hourly, dependence on the Lord. This lesson of consistent dependency on the Lord has taken time with initial and continuing periods of frustration. On the opposite end of the faith healing spectrum were and are those who do not believe in it at all. I will share one story that seems to disprove that view. My oldest sister, who recently passed, described what I consider a miraculous healing. Her daughter was stung by an insect in the backyard. She went into what I understand was anaphylactic shock. She was taken to a hospital where she was a nurse. She was on life support for days. The brain showed no activity. After tears and heartbreak, the family made the decision to cease life support. My sister, a woman of faith and prayer, had a group that she described as faith healers come in for prayer. The next day when the life support was removed, my cousin awoke. It did take some recovery period, but she is alive today. However, the Lord doesn't always answer the way we want or think He will. I remember one time when I was moving back into a closer walk with the Lord that I had a friend in the hospital dying. I knew the couple but not the whole family. I felt the Lord moving me to go to the hospital to pray for her healing even though I had been praying for her. I was scared and didn't want to do something like this publicly. When I arrived, a small group of people whom I didn't know approached me. They said, "Don't worry. We have already prayed over her, but the Lord is going to take her." I hadn't said anything to anyone about why I was there. To this day, I still don't understand exactly why the Lord wanted me to go, how they knew why I was there, or what this all means. I just know it happened, and I took a baby step in faith. I saw that the Lord's ways are not ours and that we must just act in faith and obedience but accept in faith and trust His will in matters, especially in healing.

Yes, at that time, I was perplexed. In some ways, my confusion at this time connected with my earlier discussion of how I asked my mother to spank me but not ask why. I loved my mother. I didn't want to disappoint her. I knew I had not been obedient. I thought I needed to be punished. I was not fully embracing the concept that she would be disappointed but still have the same love for me even if I disobeyed. I considered disobedience extremely serious with the Lord, which I still do. I did wonder at times if the Lord might be punishing me. Yet, I felt His love. I knew the Lord paid the price for my sin and disobedience; at least, I knew this with my head. I needed to let this fact sink into my being. I did want to please Him. I kept making mistakes. I needed to straighten out the differences in confusing teachings between the old and new covenants and works versus grace. Though I normally don't use the MSG translation, I believe it puts Hebrews 8:6–13 in easy-to-understand terms about the Old and New Covenant:

> But Jesus' priestly work far surpasses what these other priests do since he's working from a far better plan. If the first plan—the old covenant—had worked out, a second wouldn't have been needed. But we know the first was found wanting because God said:

Heads up! The days are coming

when I'll set up a new plan

for dealing with Israel and Judah.

I'll throw out the old plan

I set up with their ancestors

when I led them by the hand out of Egypt.

They didn't keep their part of the bargain,

so I looked away and let it go.

This new plan I'm making with Israel

isn't going to be written on paper,

isn't going to be chiseled in stone;

This time I'm writing out the plan *in* them,

carving it on the lining of their hearts.

I'll be their God,

they'll be my people.

They won't go to school to learn about me,

or buy a book called *God in Five Easy Lessons*.

They'll all get to know me firsthand,

the little and the big, the small and the great.

They'll get to know me by being kindly forgiven,

with the slate of their sins forever wiped clean.

By coming up with a new plan, a new covenant between God and his people, God put the old plan on the shelf. And there it stays, gathering dust.

There are some points that I don't like about this translation. God's plan was His plan from the beginning. The old covenant was to show how sin and death cannot be conquered by us. The law shows this clearly. I see more clearly now how the law and the Old Testament present what we can't achieve, what God's plan is to do about this, and how He will do it. Christ was able to do what we can't. He did it because He and the Father love us. Our debt is cleared by Christ. We *can now* receive His gift if we choose. Then, we can have that deep, personal relationship with the Lord now and forever.

I knew Christ died for my sins and that I was forgiven, but I kept hearing so much about works. It would take time for me to sift through that the works are a natural flow as fruit. I think that I might have occasionally dusted off the Old Covenant, forgetting about the fact that I was covered under the New Covenant. When I would try to perform by my own ability, I would fail miserably. I became so discouraged, disappointed in myself, thinking I had failed and would always feel shameful, a complete disgrace to my Lord. For a time, I just gave up, making things worse. However, I had my anchor. I knew the Lord loved me. I knew and felt His love. I did have my "helmet of salvation." I knew this because I knew Him and not just about Him. His patience and love would continually pull me, even though I had many scrapes and bruises along the way due to my move from just trusting Him to trying to do and understand by myself and letting the world confuse me.

As I was hurt by others, I would stray from praying for those who wronged me. I would try myself to forget and forgive but doing this was so hard by myself. I would hear and try to learn about boundaries. Sometimes I thought that I needed to just wall myself off emotionally. I even wrote companion poems about "The Wall" and "No Wall at All." I would feel my heart hardening and just couldn't let it. I believe the Lord wouldn't let it.

"The Wall"

Young and free, I saw the beauty of the rose.

I ran for its fragrance, wondering how it grows.

But as I grabbed it to see what it contained,

I felt within my hand such awful pain.

I decided right then and there,

That for lovely flowers, I wouldn't care.

I skipped along the road one day.

I saw the clover, smelled the hay.

I decided to shed my shoes, run, laugh, and play.

Tiny stickers hidden in the blades of grass,

Pricked the flesh as I ran past.

Another hurtful lesson I had learned.

To inviting fields, I would not return.

Always on the certain path, I would stay,

And always wear my shoes when out to play.

Others helped to hinder and to stifle me,

To make me fear each new possibility.

I tried one day to show my soul, my heart.

They laughed, jeered, tore my pride apart.

I learned to hide, seeking safety behind my wall.

Certain no harm could now on me befall.

A few times, I ventured out for tries at love,

Believing this was true, sent from above.

But each time, disaster was the rule,

Trapped, swept deep was I into the whirlpool.

I fought my way upward, out one more time.

Accepting that what I wanted could not be mine.

This time the wall was reinforced with despair and pain.

Never dare to go out again—my refrain.

So now, I'm safe behind my wall,

Peacefully watching sun, rain, and snowfall.

Warmed behind my wall of thickened glass.

I watch the games; the world go past.

I feel no hurt, no sorrow, grief, or pain.

But there's so much I cannot gain!

Staying safe, I cannot smell, taste, or touch,

The reality of life I want so very much.

The wall is secure, protecting me,

But inside, it's quiet, motionless—empty!

"No Wall at All"

I, too, saw the lovely rose in bloom.

Pricked my hand, saw red drops of doom.

Somehow, I went beyond the hurting in the flood.

I noticed the common color, the rose, the blood.

I felt bonding with the beauty was worth the pain.

But for partial security, I'd use some restrain.

Avoid the thorns; certainly, I would try,

But I would not let flowers pass me by.

I, also, found the stickers in my feet,

But saw it a challenge and not defeat.

I would walk the path when out to play.

But finding a weedless patch along my way,

I'd shed my shoes, wander in the grass,

Freeing my spirit from the difficult task,

Of trying to stay contained, confined

On a certain road others defined.

Like you, others tried to trap, to hamper me.

They laughed, they jeered at what I was to be.

The essence, the creativity that I had,

Strangely, their laughter only made me glad.

Somehow, I knew just who I was inside.

And if they couldn't see, I wouldn't hide.

The hurts in love were the hardest to bear.

I had so much I wanted to share.

I wondered why and today still do,

Why I can't wall myself in like you.

If I could, I might not feel the pain.

But what would I lose—hope to gain?

So burned by sun, soaked by rain and snow,

At least I am certain, I always know,

That I am alive committed to reality.

Not ever alone—never, never empty!

I do wish I understood then more about the Holy Spirit. Over time, I have learned so much about the Holy Spirit. John 14:26 (NKJV) says, "But the Helper, the Holy Spirit, whom the Father will send in My name, He will teach you all things, and bring to your remembrance all things that I said to you." I am so glad the Lord continued the pulling. I would be led to individuals strong in personal relationship with the Lord and their teaching. I would remember things that I needed to learn, understand, and embrace. I would feel His presence and love. I remember one time when I was feeling down about myself that I was sitting in my car, having left a store. Suddenly, my new pair of pearls that had been a special gift just broke for no reason. I looked at the pearls in my lap. Then, I saw a jewelry repair store out of my window. I gathered the pearls and put them in a sack from another purchase after emptying it. I went into the shop. The owner arranged the pearls on the counter. He said there should be a large one in the center. I returned to the car, looking along the way. I searched and searched but could not find it anywhere in the car. I returned to see the owner smiling. He said that he realized that he had one that would work perfectly. This was one that he had found weeks earlier. After my necklace was repaired with the new pearl, I sat again in my car. I remembered scriptures about pearls and their value. I thought about how my Lord valued me enough to die for me and how He knew the number of hairs on my head. "Aren't two sparrows sold for a penny? Yet not one of them falls to the ground apart from your Father's will. Even all the hairs on your head are numbered. So do not be afraid; you are more valuable than many sparrows" (Matthew 10:29–31, NET). With such attention to detail about me, I shouldn't fear. I felt His love as though He was telling me that He had restrung my pearls and that I, too, was of immense value and should view myself accordingly. I cried, knowing that even when I failed Him that I had been and was covered by His sacrifice and enveloped in His love. I just needed to see the truth He was telling me. I believe this was a turning point in this area of struggle. The part about not fearing was another struggle, as I would encounter many times when fear would creep in or appear with and without warning.

Warnings and Protection

The statutes of the LORD *are* right, rejoicing
the heart;
The commandment of the LORD *is* pure,
enlightening the eyes;

The fear of the LORD *is* clean, enduring forever;
The judgments of the LORD *are* true *and* righ-
teous altogether.

More to be desired are they than gold,
Yea, than much fine gold;
Sweeter also than honey and the honeycomb.
Moreover by them Your servant is warned,
And in keeping them there is great reward.

Psalm 19:8–11 (NKJV)

"Warnings"

The thick clouds gather slowly, darkening with rain.

The wind belts forth as force it quickly starts to gain.

These are the warning signs of a storm suddenly to come.

We learn by trial and error where danger signals emit from.

But there are traps and pits that are so hard to see.

Failing to watch, we're caught and struggle to get free.

We may not have the knowledge or the wisdom to escape the hurt.

Without discernment, we lack the skill and strength dangers to avert.

How many times did You warn me before I asked Your aid?

How many times did You save me when I was lost and afraid?

How did You teach and show me Your messages and signs to read?

How can You prepare with such love and care for my every need?

Much of the time, I was unaware of sudden dangers and the Lord's protection from dangers. As I look back on some, I realize that I may have had warnings, even if I didn't realize it at the time. There are many of these, but I will share a few. When I was young, I remember a night when the window was opened with just the screen for protection. My sister, closest to my age, and I slept together. I preferred the side of the bed close to the window because it was cooler. I woke one night and, for some reason, slightly opened my eyes. I saw a man's face looking in the window. I closed my eyes with that image still in my mind. In fact, I can close my eyes and still see that face today. I was scared but didn't know what to do. I wondered if there was space enough between the bed and the window to roll off onto the floor and go under the bed so I could run to my parents' room. I am surprised that I considered doing this because I had fears that something was under the bed, like alligators. I would sometimes jump off the foot of the bed at a distance if I had to go to the bathroom during the night so the monsters under the bed couldn't get me. Could a real fear have overruled an imaginary one? Then, I thought that my sister would still be in bed. I didn't know what to do. I said in my mind what I have said so many times since, both aloud and in my mind, "Help me, Jesus!"

The phone rang. I heard a noise outside the window and the sound of my mother going to answer the phone. I opened my eyes, and the face was gone, but a figure was going away. The call was from a neighbor across the street who had seen the person and called to alert my parents. I don't know his intent, if he was dangerous or just a "peeping Tom" as I heard people call such individuals. I know I was scared.

As a teen, I felt a nudging not to go to certain places or gatherings. For example, a group wanted me to go with them after a home-coming decoration session for the upcoming football game. I didn't. I know they didn't really mean any harm. However, they went to the opposing team's school to put up signs. The police arrived, and all involved had unfortunate encounters not only with the police but also with parents and our school administrators. A more serious incident was when I was driving to a class when I was starting college. I thought I would take a shortcut to save time. This shortcut included a dark, lonely street with a train crossing. Of course, a train came, blocking the road. For some reason, I felt not to come too close to the tracks and to look at my rearview mirror. At a short distance behind me, I saw a car with the driver's and passenger's doors open. Two men were approaching my car. I quickly made a turn-around, thanks to the space I had allowed between me and the tracks. I think I did this so fast that I shocked the men so that I managed to leave that road without hitting them or further incident. One would think that that incident would have taught me a lesson. However, years later, as an adult, I was tempted and took a shortcut through a dark park. At a stop sign in the park, my car stalled. I saw a group of individuals walking toward my car from out of the park. True, I cannot say for certain that they meant me any harm. I prayed aloud, and my car started just in time to avert their arrival. To this day, I avoid shortcuts that have lonely, dark, or dangerous areas. If I am alone, I may even take a less pleasant drive with traffic, longer distance, and more time-consuming. I connect my phone to one of my son's so he can track me when I go to his house. Once I stopped too long at a location because there was a line for gas and a line for the bathroom. I was already in his town. He called to check that all was okay. The Lord not only warns and protects but also provides others for our protection.

Although the situations that I have mentioned thus far may or may not have been life-threatening, some I have experienced were. In early August of 1985, I was scheduled to go to a meeting. I felt uneasy about the time of the meeting and not the meeting itself. I lived close to DFW Airport. I felt that sense of warning that I had learned to trust. I canceled the meeting, rescheduling for a later date. I immediately had personal peace but still some sense of concern. If I had kept the appointment, I would have been on Highway 114 exactly at the time of the Delta 191 crash. As it was, I did hear the horrible sounds of what resulted in the loss of life of so many that day, including one driving on Highway 114 that evening. I have had a number of warnings about flights. Some, the Lord willing, I will write about in a future book. Another warning that came in a feeling of uneasiness occurred after my daughter had her keys to her car stolen. The house key was also on that key ring. I was unable to have the house door locks changed until the next day. I awoke and knew I needed to be alert. I went into the living room and sat in the dark. The front door had a glass section in it, and through it, I could see a figure approaching the door in the dark. I turned the front light on and shouted. The individual ran away. This incident reminded me of one when my children were young. I would sit in the dark in the morning, having my coffee and quiet time. I heard someone working on the door and window, trying to gain entry. I screamed and quickly called the police because there had been several houses broken into in the area. I know that these could seem like coincidences to people.

Later, I would have clear warnings that came in threes and through scriptures. These would also prove to show powerful protection. I found that in one week that I encountered the same scripture appearing in devotional reading, broadcasts, and in a study I was doing. The verse was: "Then your light shall break forth like the morning, Your healing shall spring forth speedily, And your righteousness shall go before you; The glory of the LORD shall be your rear guard" (Isaiah 58:8, NKJV). I wondered about this seeming coincidence but didn't really think about applying it to me other than thinking how beautiful this verse was and how wonderful the Lord's promises and protection are. I was driving home from church and was at a stop sign waiting my turn when a tall truck speeded from behind, crashing into my car. Both vehicles were totaled. The police officer insisted I go to the hospital, although I felt fine. He said, "With so much damage to these vehicles, I am certain that you have some injuries." I thought about my week of warning coupled with a promise, "The glory of the Lord shall be your (my) rear guard." The doctor at the hospital couldn't find anything wrong with me but said I would certainly need the pain pills he prescribed. I never needed them. It would be years later that I learned about how the Lord can provide a special *rhema* word. I knew some about this Greek word from Plato and Aristotle, who used it when speaking of propositions. I have learned that this word denotes in scripture how the Holy Spirit can use scripture or a part of it to speak a special word to a believer for a specific situation or reason. I have learned so much from seeing Hebrew and Greek in scriptures. Even though I am just a beginner with these, I have found that my years studying other languages has been meaningful in helping me understand translations and original meanings. The Greek *rhema* and *logos* can both mean *word*. I found the scriptures that use *rhema* helpful in understanding how important it is to hear, understand, and act upon not just all scripture but especially those instances of *rhema* for me personally. John 6:63 (NKJV) says, "It is the Spirit who gives life; the flesh profits nothing. The words (*rhema*) that I speak to you are spirit, and they are life." When Jesus was tempted by Satan in the wilderness, He answered using scripture, "But He answered and said, "It is written, 'Man shall not live by bread alone, but by every word *(rhema)* that proceeds from the mouth of God'" (Matthew 4:4, NKJV). When I looked back at the scripture in Deuteronomy 8, I found that the Hebrew indicates, "every *motza* that comes out of the Lord's mouth" (*kol morza pi* Adonai). I am still asking for more understanding. However, I am realizing that I need to feed on the Lord's Word and listen to the Holy Spirit so that I can hear what I am to know. This incident helped to build in me a confidence that His word is living and vital to me and offers warnings, protections, and knowledge. I know that these need to be confirmed and not just my own imagination. I have found comfort in the three occurrences prior to the incident and am learning to seek scripture to confirm. I am sharing to testify of the greatness of the Lord. Here are two more scripture that use *rhema* although there are many more:

> "So then faith cometh by hearing, and hearing by the word (*rhema*) of God" (Romans 10:17, KJV).

> "And take the helmet of salvation, and the sword of the Spirit, which is the word (*rhema*) of God" (Ephesians 6:17, KJV).

Another occasion when I received a warning was preceded by a reoccurring dream as well as the same scripture appearing in reading, devotional, and radio messages. The dream showed a dark snake slithering through the flower beds. I awoke one of the times wondering about why I was having this dream. The scriptures I kept encountering also had to do with snakes. It was from Numbers 21. The children of Israel, although miraculously freed from slavery in Egypt, began to speak against God and Moses because they were discouraged. Fiery serpents began to bite people, so many died. The people repented for what they said and implored Moses to pray to God, which he did.

> Then the LORD said to Moses, "Make a fiery serpent, and set it on a pole; and it shall be that everyone who is bitten, when he looks at it, shall live." So Moses made a bronze serpent, and put it on a pole; and so it was, if a serpent had bitten anyone, when he looked at the bronze serpent, he lived.
>
> **Numbers 21:8–9 (NKJV)**

I admit that I wondered if the Lord was trying to tell me something. One evening when I was watering the flower bed, I felt a sharp, yes fiery, pain in my foot. I dropped the hose and ran into the house. I saw two punctures on the top of my foot. I could see through the glass of the back door a large dark snake acting like it was trying to get into the house. I immediately prayed, "Lord, I don't know where that bronze serpent on a staff is, but I look to you for my health and safety." Shortly afterward, I would see the connection between prophecy and Christ's death on the cross with the scripture that I had been given. I guess I needed to learn in stages. Recently, I studied the Hebrew word for looked, deciding that I like Young's Literal Translation for Numbers 21:9 (preferring *make* instead of *maketh*, set not *setteth*, and *has* in place of *hath*): "And Moses maketh a serpent of brass, and setteth it on the ensign, and it hath been, if the serpent hath bitten any man, and he hath looked expectingly unto the serpent of brass—he hath lived." I am understanding that we do need to "look expectingly" when we hold on to His word when seeking protection. My husband and next-door neighbor killed the snake that was aggressive as they killed it. On the way to the hospital, I called my sister and a dear friend. I had learned by this time the power of prayer warriors. My sister, my friend, and my friend's husband arrived at the hospital almost as soon as I did. Thank the Lord that they did. The hospital seemed uncertain exactly what to think. My two supporters saw I was going into shock and that the nurse was not finding my vein. In fairness, I have tiny veins that crawl. I am always grateful when medical personnel can find them without too much difficulty. My husband took the doctor to the truck to show him the snake for identification—cottonmouth water moccasin. I don't remember much after this until

I would later leave in the early morning hours. I know my friend sent her husband to get extra blankets, and she and my sister played a leading role in directing activity until the doctor came in; I believe I must have gone into shock from what I was told. Observably was a blob of venom trapped in a little pocket on my foot. I would recover without problem, although the two little punctures were visible for some time. I remembered an incident with the same foot. I had been bitten by a recluse spider on my big toe. I know we had seen them in the house during that time. I didn't realize it at first, but I went to see a podiatrist. I had a hard knot on my big toe. He had to cut away what seemed like a hard shell. He was surprised to find a liquid that he thought was venom inside. He mentioned that he thought he had heard of some horses doing this, encapsulating venom. After treatment, I was fine. This event happened before I had begun my tutorials with the Lord to return to a closer relationship again and that daily searching of the scriptures that I did as a youth. I did thank the Lord, keenly aware of His protection.

A situation that arose after I saw again how important it is to daily seek the Lord, His scriptures, and His will was after I had been to a chiropractor who had taken X-rays. He was alarmed at the condition of my neck. He showed me the X-ray and explained the problem. I was scheduled to begin some treatment in a couple of weeks. I just didn't have peace about this and sought not my guidance but the Lord's. I prayed. I read scriptures. I prayed more. I read more. Finally, the day arrived when I was to begin treatment. I still had no peace. In desperation, I prayed, "Lord, please show me something or give me peace." I opened my Bible to a scripture I am ashamed to say I don't think I had read before. I did know another section of this chapter in Proverbs. It was Proverbs 3:21–22 (NKJV), "My son, let them not depart from your eyes—Keep sound wisdom and discretion; So they will be life to your soul And grace to your neck." When I read these verses, I had my *rhema* even though I didn't know about that Greek word and its significance at that time. I suddenly felt peace. I called, canceling my appointment. I didn't think anymore about my neck until a few years later when I went to a different chiropractor. He did X-rays prior to our formal consultation. I asked him how bad my neck was. He looked puzzled and said that my neck was okay. I see this as the Lord giving me grace for my neck. This doctor would become a great Christian friend and wonderful medical caregiver. This doctor has helped me many times. Once was when I fell down the stairs. I was alone because my

husband was working out of town. I remember thinking, "Dear Lord, keep me conscious and allow me to get
to my phone." I did. A wonderful neighbor took me to
this doctor. Because of the myasthenia gravis, I usually
avoid pain medication and muscle relaxers. He was able
to help me deal with the pain using acupuncture, heat-
ed cups, a special belt, and instructions on how best to
walk. The pain was severe, so his being able to do these
things to manage the pain was wonderful. The Lord provided him, my neighbor, and a guitar stand that I used to
get up from the one chair I could sit in and from the toi-
let. Also, I used the guitar stand to put my laptop on so
that I could continue to work from home. I don't play the
guitar and didn't even have one, but some of my grandsons do. For some reason, a guitar stand had been left at
my house. Looking back, I laugh at the Lord's provision
and sense of humor. One of my sons stopped by on his
way out of town and rigged a clothes rack and exercise
pulls so that I could manage to get in and out of bed. I
kept it that way for several years as a reminder. I only
recently removed it with the help of the same son. After
I improved some, I needed to go out of town but wasn't
comfortable driving. My dear neighbor took me to the
airport. The Lord protected both of us. We were coming out from an overpass when a huge tire like those on

eighteen-wheelers came crashing down. It did do some damage to the car, but we were uninjured. Both Psalm 91 and all of the previously mentioned Proverbs 3 would become important to my life as the Lord would continue to help me grow in faith, protect me, and provide for me.

These later warnings were different from the ones that I had received earlier. These warnings connected me with scriptures and produced a strong trust in the Lord and a desire to stay attuned to what the Lord was saying to and teaching me. The earlier ones were often experienced as a feeling of uneasiness. This feeling, as I learned to mature in the Lord, was seen more as a lack of peace that would lead to searching scriptures and prayer. One experience might be what I call a midway one. It was initiated by a feeling of certainty within a grim time, followed by a lack of peace several times later, followed by more peace. I had been ill and unable to work. My myasthenia gravis often meant that flu shots and/or such illnesses themselves could take me months to recover fully to prior strength. During one of these episodes, I received a call from a woman whom I didn't know who had seen me deliver a workshop in another state. She wanted me to go with her to Ukraine. I said, "Yes," without even thinking about it, and had experienced perfect peace. My quick response and peace made no logical sense, given my health situation at the time. I would travel to New York to meet with people I didn't know and go with them. There were many experiences during this trip. Most will be told in a future book (the Lord willing). However, I wish to share one here. Often, the locals would take us to see a few unique sites in the area where we would be holding workshops. Our group was treated to a visit to the former resident and a small museum dedicated to a poet who had shown patriotism and bravery with her work. The grounds were lovely, and her house had an almost eerie atmosphere that she was there, still composing and lamenting. The museum visit was a shock for me. As I looked at pictures and writings hung along a long room, I was aware that people were staring at me. Was something wrong with my slip, my skirt, my face, or my hair? I noticed they were looking at a long painting at the end of the room and then at me. I walked toward the painting, feeling very conspicuous. Then, I saw what was piquing their curiosity. A water nymph in the picture looked like how I looked at that time. I felt great relief when we exited the museum and were once again on the quiet but lovely grounds. Later that day, we were invited to a celebration of the summer solstice at the river that evening. I quickly declined. I am not sure why I knew that I was not to go. Maybe I just needed the rest, or maybe I was avoiding something that would have been dangerous for me. I said earlier that many events during my trips to Ukraine were ones that I experienced warnings, opportunities, and protections. This one was unique in that all I know is that I sensed a quick warning followed by a rush of peace when I declined the invitation.

Another event when I was keenly aware of protection was while driving. Freeways and their exits can be concerning and dangerous in my area. I was on such a freeway and was about to exit when a tall truck sped across the lanes toward me. In a split second, I remember thinking, *This is it*, and *Help me, Lord*. Then, it seemed as though I was in a movie where I was at a very slowed speed, but the action in front of me continued at a regular speed. All I knew was I was saved from what could have been a deadly accident. I thanked the Lord. I realize that these last two events seem vague and ambiguous to the reader. Those thoughts are okay. However, for me, these are times when I sensed the presence of the Lord, directing and protecting. I am learning each day to have ears to hear and eyes to see. Recently, as I have been writing, I had an early morning scare and trip in an ambulance to the hospital that was a warning that I see as a blessing. I knew something was terribly wrong. My husband called 911. When personnel arrived, my blood pressure was 30/60. At my age, they assumed a heart issue. Although not very strong or clear-headed, I thought I should laugh when I heard in the ambulance, "Your heart is fine." I heard this same phrase from the doctor at the hospital. I thought, *Oh, what a blessing to know my heart is fine because I had wondered if that was the problem.* I discovered that I had gallstones. Oh, what a blessed warning. I could now take measures by diet and medication to try to dissolve them. It is best with my myasthenia gravis if I avoid anesthesia, so surgery would not be the best option. Yes, I am learning, though it has taken me years to move into this place, that walking in the Spirit requires my consent and openness to listen, see, and follow. I try to remember when I begin driving to pray for protection and attention on my part and those around me. Oh, that I would be increasingly attuned and obedient, but I am not there yet.

In Times of Trouble

Therefore do not worry about tomorrow, for tomorrow will worry about its own things. Sufficient for the day is its own trouble.

Matthew 6:34 (NKJV)

Who comforts us in all our tribulation, that we may be able to comfort those who are in any trouble, with the comfort with which we ourselves are comforted by God.

2 Corinthians 1:4 (NKJV)

Let not your heart be troubled; you believe in God, believe also in Me. In My Father's house are many mansions; if it were not so, I would have told you. I go to prepare a place for you. And if I go and prepare a place for you, I will come again and receive you to Myself; that where I am, there you may be also. And where I go you know, and the way you know.

Thomas said to Him, "Lord, we do not know where You are going, and how can we know the way?"

Jesus said to him, "I am the way, the truth, and the life. No one comes to the Father except through Me. "

John 14:1–6 (NKJV)

"What Do I Do?"

Love slipped away one lonely day.
Life lost all of its meaning.
Love slipped away one sad day.
I need a shoulder for leaning.

Crashed down to the ground,
Tormented all around,
I look to You!
What do I do?

Dreams faded from my eyes.
Memories linger now.
Teardrops glisten with goodbyes.
Life continues, but how?

Crashed down to the ground,
Tormented all around,
I look to You!
What do I do?

The future pained by times past.
First hopes can no longer be.

Nothing in this world seems to last.

Only heartache now can I see.

Crashed down to the ground,

Tormented all around,

I look to You!

What do I do?

I selected several scriptures for this chapter and would have liked to have added many more. In times of trouble, I have found that each situation is different and different scriptures provide the comfort or wisdom needed. Unfortunately, I did not always seek out these scriptures, or at least not in time. Many of my troubles were because I sought my own wisdom, the advice of those who weren't attuned to the Lord's wisdom, or rejected what I should have done. Some troubles were the result of others in my life making decisions that were not in my interest; some troubles were ones that life simply provides. I sometimes need to remind myself what Jesus said about tribulations (troubles), "These things I have spoken to you, that in Me you may have peace. In the world, you will have tribulation; but be of good cheer, I have overcome the world" (John 16:33, NKJV). Another word in scriptures that I connect with these two is trials. I have learned that by looking to the Lord for understanding from these experiences, I can be of help to others and grow in patience. (Corinthians 1:4 and James 1:2–8) I can't begin to list all the times that I believed that I experienced trouble, and many of these that seemed major at the time were mere bumps in retrospect. I will share a few from which I learned much and especially experienced the Lord's presence.

I always wanted to have children. I had a fear as a teen that, for some reason, I might not, even though I had a name already if I had a girl. My first pregnancy seemed like a completely normal one, and I had a notable obstetrician. I was completing my last semester of undergraduate studies. Everything was going well, except one of my professors had written that my dress was not as professional as necessary. I was preparing to perform student teaching in the fall as the last step to adding teacher certification to my record. I had made what I considered appropriate clothing. However, I was concealing what today's women often accentuate as their baby bump. This negative was removed from my record when the Dean explained to the professor that I was pregnant. I do remember a time in the latter stages of my pregnancy when I awoke with a deep sense of sadness. I have wondered if that was the actual moment that the baby passed. My next appointment showed no sign of a heartbeat. The doctor tried another stethoscope. Then, he had me wait in the office for an hour. I could tell he was concerned. He had called my husband and a family member to come to the office. He repeated listening, but there was still no heartbeat. I don't remember much more after this second examination because I was crying and distraught. I was glad that he had called support for me. Procedures and options were much different than they are today. His advice was that we wait awhile before doing anything, monitoring me frequently to ensure nothing would negatively impact my health. He said that if we could avoid surgery that future pregnancies would be easier for me. I was an emotional wreck. If I went anywhere trying to keep my mind away from my sadness and sense of loss, people would see that I was very pregnant and ask when the baby was due. I would burst into tears. I couldn't be around family without crying because my cousins had new babies. We had to take down the baby crib and the items arranged in the nursery for the baby's arrival. After a few weeks, the doctor decided to do a new procedure to induce labor. I am not certain exactly what it was, but I later learned that it is no longer used. Nurses and doctors lined the walls of my hospital room. I had agreed to allow these witnesses because this was a new procedure. However, it was a little terrifying to see them. Again, I don't remember much until I woke up in recovery. Unfortunately, the first one to question me was a nurse asking for a name for the little boy for the death certificate. This was the first I was to know that it was a little boy. We didn't have all the opportunities then to know the sex of the baby prior to birth. I began to sob uncontrollably, and she left. A familiar face appeared. A young man with whom I went to high school and had dated a couple of times was there. His family owned a funeral home. He kindly consoled me and told me that his family would take care of everything and not worry. Soon, I had family there to help me. I would still be in the hospital when the graveside service was held. My husband was with me. I believe it would have been too painful for either of us to attend the service. This stillbirth occurred at the height of the Vietnam Conflict. My husband had an exemption first because of marriage and then because of my pregnancy. Almost immediately, the government changed his status, and he opted to join a service. I left our house and moved in with my parents. My emotions were still raw as I often awoke, thinking that I could hear my baby crying. I did begin my student teaching in the fall. The demands really helped my emotional healing. One thing that I must share is that I had the Great Comforter during all this time. I felt the love and presence of my Lord. I don't think I could have endured it without Him. I thought of scriptures about David's sorrow and prayers for his baby. I was comforted by his words that he would see his child again. I knew that my baby was safe with the Lord and that I would have that reunion one day. I never blamed the Lord because, as a child, I knew His love for me and felt His love to carry me through this troubled time.

My next pregnancy would be anything but normal. I don't know if it was pregnancy itself or the environment. I had joined my husband for the last phase of some training. I was told we would be in a cottage by a pond. It turned out to be a shack by a mosquito shallow. I had never seen a half bathtub before. I had to cross my legs to take a bath. I had to be certain to put lids on pots and pans because the ceiling paint was peeling, and I didn't want it in the food. I ironed on a closed suitcase. The closest phone was at a little grocery about a block away from the small collection of shacks. I had just graduated college but found myself around teen wives who had many superstitions. I learned much during this time but felt lonely. One day, I drove to a washeteria and met a lovely woman. We talked and talked, excited to have someone with some shared experiences. I would go back there a few times but never saw her again. One night when the husbands all had to stay on base, I heard my dog Pepe barking frantically. Then, I heard a pounding on the door. When I opened it, the wives from the few other isolated shacks ran in, telling me to lock the door because someone was trying to get them. They had gathered at the place next to mine for the night; I had declined. I am not certain why they came to me, but they did. Someone had tried to break into

117

the back where they were. My dog continued to snarl and bark, now at my back door. I handed out my set of butcher knives that I had received as a wedding present. I shouted a warning. I directed our defense procedures if anyone broke through. Finally, all was quiet, even my dog. When morning came, and it was time for the little store to open, we prepared our trip to it so that we could call the police (none of us had a phone, and remember, there were no cellphones). Each of us, armed with our own butcher knife, walked together to the little store in a manner to guard all directions. It must have been a county sheriff who arrived from the look of the uniform. He said we had done correct things and noted that one of the other places had shown signs of a break-in attempt. I assumed the Lord protected us all. I was grateful. However, when the officer told us that if we had to kill someone to drag him inside, I was shocked. Oh, what a horrible thought! Fortunately, I was to see not only that we were being helped and protected but also that the Lord provided a wonderful church in nearby Memphis. By the time we were inside the church during our first visit, people knew where we were from and located members for us to meet from our hometown. By the end of the service (Sunday), someone had an appointment for me to interview for a teaching position the next week. We were taken to lunch at a couple's expense. This church seemed attuned to each other and to the Lord. I don't believe I have experienced such care since then, especially from a large congregation. The pastor's wife continued to write me for several years to keep in contact with us. This support contrasted with the feeling of fear and rejection from others. Martin Luther King Jr. was assassinated on April 4, 1968, in Memphis. Anger was a part of the atmosphere. I remember driving alone in Memphis and having angry individuals trying to stop my car. I drove through this as quickly as possible. I do believe the Lord must have helped me escape what seemed an extremely dangerous situation. I was not used to racial conflict of this nature because I had been reared to accept others and had friends in a variety of racial and social groups. I felt that I saw hatred for me in some eyes even though I didn't know and had done nothing wrong to them. Soon, we were sent to a naval air station where different issues would arise.

Because we had limited funds in our new location, I applied for teaching opportunities. I enrolled in a nearby university to add another course to my resume, hoping it would help me acquire a permanent position in the fall. However, this attempt was short-lived but showed me how the Lord could orchestrate incidents for our good. I realized after having to stop the car en route to throw up that I was pregnant again. As I sat on a bench outside the administration building on campus, I noticed a woman who was distraught and in tears. I went to her to ask if I could help in any way. She had completed everything necessary for her teaching degree, but the French course that she just knew that she would certainly fail. I told her that French was one of my majors and that I would be glad to help her. She said that she didn't have much money. I told her not to worry. She and her family became dear friends. Her family often shared meals with us when we were in need and later would provide babysitting. This meeting was only one of many happenings that I know the Lord orchestrated.

We were now in a hot, humid climate in the summertime and living in an unairconditioned trailer. I made a swimsuit to cover my emerging baby bump and would often use a water hose outside to drench myself so that I could stand the heat inside to cook or do housework. I met a woman in the trailer park who had a toddler. I bartered babysitting in exchange for a porta crib and some baby clothes. The Lord was definitely helping me out. Most notably, I remember praying for clouds to cool down the trailer on extremely hot, humid days. My prayers were answered. Yes, I remembered to pray about everything! Finally, we were able to secure base housing, although it was not much better but a little cooler. We had one side of a duplex with no doors on the cabinets or closets and an exposed hot water heater. We did have large, screened windows and an old but exceptionally large bathtub. I did manage to become a grader for a professor at a nearby college, which helped some with expenses. He would bring papers to me and then pick them up. Even using the commissary, we still had to be careful with money. At least I was not having to share crackers and peanut butter with the dog any longer or divide up a can of fruit so that I would have some for several days. I remember a time when my husband was to be gone for several days at sea that I had truly little money. I had enough gas to drive to a relative's house who lived in a town not too far away. It was a nice break to be in air conditioning, have good meals, and even be taken a few places. I received a little extra money from them and a full tank of gas. On a stretch of road where there was nothing and no other cars, my car threw a rod (I learned that fact later). I was stranded. Of course, this was before cellphones. I prayed. The Lord answered. A patrol car appeared. They offered to call a taxi for me. However, when they checked the price of the taxi from my current location to the base, I realized

I didn't have enough money. They were so nice. They loaded me, my small bag, barking chihuahua, and the one nice maternity dress that I had made into the patrol car. No sooner than we were in the car than they received a call about a shooting. They headed toward the location. There were several patrol cars and active shooting in a field when we arrived at the scene. A man in uniform, whom I assumed was higher ranking than my officers, shined a flashlight in the back, which action started my dog barking. He learned about my situation and moved me into his vehicle. It was the early morning hours when the officer dropped me off at the base guard gate. I felt embarrassed by the looks the guards gave me as I carried my dog, bag, and dress through the gate after exiting a police car. Fortunately, my duplex was just inside the gate. I thought my rescue was complete, but I was wrong. I went inside tired and sore from the experience. I decided to take a long, hot bath. I filled the tub with water and laid back. At first, the bath felt so good. However, the water grew cooler, and the wind was blowing in from the window above the tub. As I tried to get out, I realized my pregnant body would not, and my foot could not reach the knob to turn warm water back on. I began to yell for help. My dog started barking. It seemed like some time before help arrived. I was extremely embarrassed this time and vowed to myself not to do anything else that could require a rescue. Fortunately, a kindly mechanic and his wife were able to help retrieve and repair the car. I am not sure I understood as much at the time how the Lord had provided for us and used others to do so. Now, I am faster to see His hand and say a much quicker thank you.

Incidents with this pregnancy were still to come. I was in a long checkout line at the commissary when I must have fainted. I came to later only to see that people had moved me and my basket aside so that they could move forward. I was struck by the difference in reaction from this group as compared to the concern that I received from the other episodes. I never went to the commissary again. My due date approached, as did Christmas. I remember thinking how wonderful it would be to have a child born on Christmas Day. The event that happened that time was that my water broke. We went to the base hospital. Because we lived only about a block from there, I was told to go home and wait for labor pains. The hospital was busy and short-staffed. A few days later, I noticed a little blood and immediately went to the hospital. I remember the nurse shouting, "Oh no! I can see the baby's head!" She ran into the hall. A doctor who was walking through the hospital from playing tennis came running into the room. I believe he cleaned and gloved his hands but admit that I am not entirely certain he had time. A few hard contractions and pushes (I am not clear about all of this because I was traumatized by all that was happening and the memory of my stillbirth) brought forth my baby daughter. All seemed fine. I had planned to have a spinal or something; however, there had been no time for that. My baby girl did not seem to like being away from me. I remember that she constantly cried if she were not beside me. The corpsmen decided they would just leave her with me in bed. I worried some that I would fall asleep and hurt her. I nursed her even though the accepted trend at that time was not to do so. I thought that with limited funds and help, at least we would both have food. I did notice that my uterus seemed to contract when she nursed. I ate better because I wanted her nourished and could move her from the porta crib to nurse without getting out of bed or having to heat anything. I became an expert at changing her diaper while nursing so that I could return her fed and dry to the porta crib but keeping my hand on her so she knew I was near. I was truly blessed and moved from the base pediatrician to one in town when he told me to oil her three times a day. I met a wonderful doctor who had five children of her own, volunteered one day a week for a free clinic outside of town, and only charged me a ridiculously small amount. Once, she even offered to come to me if a child did not improve. She talked to me without agitation over the phone. Most importantly, she was okay with nursing and even rocking. I did have to make another trip to the base hospital with my daughter. She was walking by this time. She seemed not to be able to breathe and was turning blue. I ran the short distance to the hospital. This was the beginning of allergies that had not been apparent while she was nursed. She was allergic to eggs. The woman pediatrician guided me through determining and desensitizing her to many allergies. The Lord definitely carried us through and provided for us during these times.

The next episode with my daughter and little chihuahua, who helped with her and later children, occurred because of a hurricane. My husband was to go out with equipment because of the approaching storm. Initially, it was thought that it would not be bad. I became more uneasy. I felt a strong nudging by what I later realized was the Spirit guiding me. I called a helpline and connected with a family at another base inland. I packed important papers, pictures, memorabilia, supplies, baby, and dog into my car. The wind was picking up as I drove out of town. My car made a strange noise, but I prayed and kept going. Emergency vehicles passed me going into town. I reached an agreed meeting place as I drove into the next town. A lovely military family met me and took in my baby, dog, and me. They provided comfort and support. I was to learn that what was a mild storm became a major hurricane. Where I had lived, though old, survived, although water had blown through all the walls and everything inside was lost. Most new buildings had not survived. As I had no place to return to and as power was not expected to return for a couple of weeks, I left to go home to my parents' house. I had been resupplied with items needed for the journey by the family. I am reminded of the scripture in Matthew 25:35–40 (NKJV).

> Then the King will say to those on His right hand, "Come, you blessed of My Father, inherit the kingdom prepared for you from the foundation of the world: for I was hungry and you gave Me food; I was thirsty and you gave Me drink; I was a stranger and you took Me in; I *was* naked and you clothed Me; I was sick and you visited Me; I was in prison and you came to Me." Then the righteous will answer Him, saying, "Lord, when did we see You hungry and feed *You,* or thirsty and give *You* drink? When did we see You a stranger and take *You* in,

or naked and clothe *You?* Or when did we see You sick, or in prison, and come to You?" And the King will answer and say to them, "Assuredly, I say to you, in as much as you did *it* to one of the least of these My brethren, you did *it* to Me."

This couple certainly reflected such a spirit. I believe I will meet them again in Heaven because they served the Lord by serving me.

With Federal relief funding and loans, we were able to purchase some new furniture (only the baby bed frame, one bookcase, and kitchen table and chairs were salvageable). We moved off base and further from the coast. (This seemed positive but would produce an ironic twist later.) I was pregnant again. I got larger sooner. I still had to go to the base for this pregnancy. At one visit, I was told there was no heartbeat. I tried to ask calmly if the doctor was going to use a different stethoscope and then have me wait for a little, remembering the procedure when I had the stillbirth. He became frustrated with me and said, "No! Come back in one month." I left in tears and went straight to the Company Squadron Commander's office. I was on his wives' committee and knew him to be a good and just man. He saw me in tears, asked what had happened, and immediately called someone at the hospital. I was to return and see a different doctor. This doctor heard the heartbeat was fine. I don't know if it is true or not, but I heard the first doctor was removed from seeing patients. I began to see how the Lord works in advance to prepare for our needs. If I had not been on that committee, I would have had little recourse and would have suffered emotionally for at least a month.

This experience was not the last of the troubling issues with this pregnancy. As I mentioned previously, the baby was growing larger faster this time, although I seemed to be losing weight. The possibility of twins was mentioned. Of course, twins would be a blessing, but my daughter was still a toddler. Next came a tropical storm. At first, I thought that at least it wasn't a full-fledged hurricane. This storm moved slowly, dropping substantial amounts of rain. I was warned by the base that those close to delivery dates might go into labor with the passing of the storm. Surely enough, I began to have regular pains that increased in intensity. My husband, trying to get to me, mistakenly drove into the water so deep that he had to exit the car through the windows. The car had to be replaced because of water damage. An ambulance was called. I was in an upstairs apartment. I went to the inside stairwell with my daughter to watch some water rising. A man was there as well. I told him, "I am going into labor. Can you stay here until the ambulance arrives?" I can't begin to describe the look of shock on his face. He said nothing but went downstairs, wading out through the water. Two emergency personnel arrived to carry my daughter and me through the water for a little over a block. I noticed a dipsy dumpster floating. It took a while to navigate drivable streets to arrive at the base hospital. Not long afterward, the friend that I had made during the crying French event arrived to take my daughter. Left alone on a bed to wait for my contractions to intensify, I had to call a nurse. I explained to her, "I'm all wet!" The nurse said, "Oh, your water broke!" I replied, "No, the ceiling is leaking!" The bed was moved, and buckets were placed under leaks. As the storm passed, my contractions decreased. The situation was not pleasant because many of the toilets in the hospital had backed up. Personnel were busy. Food, drink, and toilets were not readily available because of the effects of the tropical storm. I pleaded after a day to be allowed to leave with the warning that I would return in less than a week. Glad to have one less to care for, they released me. I went to my friend's house first. Because our apartment was upstairs, it suffered no water damage. As soon as the water resided and a vehicle was secured,

I went home for what would be a month past my due date. I woke up one morning and started fixing breakfast. I had a hard contraction. We immediately left for the hospital. I arrived and was put on a bed in a hallway while my husband checked me in. I was checked and immediately wheeled into delivery and delivered before my husband could return. I counted about eighteen hard contractions. A baby boy was born. A very large boy, such that the doctor told me that it was lucky I had him quickly. Even with the quick birth, he had tiny indentions that the doctor said were the result of his size and the pressure. I had some ripping and had to have stitches, making the recovery a little more painful. The corpsmen loved him, calling him monster baby. This time the baby was not left with me except to nurse. I think that from listening to them that they liked caring for him. It was painful changing my sheets. Oh, did I mention that in the base hospital that one received only one clean sheet daily. Therefore, I had to take off the bottom sheet for laundry pick up, move what had been the top sheet to replace the removed bottom sheet, and use the clean sheet I had received to replace the top one. My stitches were ripped once when the nurse tried to insert a suppository in the wrong place. It was a relief to leave the hospital even though I had a toddler, a newborn, and some discomfort. I would never have to go back there again as my husband's service time was ending. Even though I was not as conscious of it then as I am now, the Lord was taking care of me and mine, giving me His peace within the storm. I can see clearly His message that said, "I have told you all this so that you may have peace in me. Here on earth, you will have many trials and sorrows. But take heart because I have overcome the world" (John 16:33, NLT).

Several events that were trying occurred prior to the birth of my next child. Some of these included deaths of family members, a miscarriage, and pneumonia. I was teaching at this time and had continued working until the end of the week, although I felt increasingly worse. My two children were asleep, my husband was working that night, and I was trying to take medicine to keep my fever down. My temperature rose anyway, I couldn't speak, and I felt very strange. I called my parents' house, but I couldn't talk. They would hang up. I kept calling. Finally, my dad came over to my house. After I let him in, he realized I was terribly ill. He called the doctor and described my symptoms. I am not certain exactly why, but the doctor arrived at the house. My dad stayed with the sleeping children, and the doctor rushed me in his car to a nearby hospital. I don't remember everything.

However, I was told that I had stopped breathing, and the doctor had to pull over to get me breathing again. I do remember treatment in the hospital, especially the breathing treatments and oxygen. I stayed there for several days, perhaps a week. When I came home, I remember how sensitive I was to sound. It wasn't long after this illness that I had a miscarriage. I don't know if it was related to being ill or not. I am thankful for the Christian doctor and my dad, who came to my rescue. I am most thankful to the Lord for sending them.

Of course, having children means mishaps and sometimes frightful events. My oldest son, when he was small, was highly active and creative. Once he hid so well in the house that I thought he had gotten outside and left without my knowing it. I had the whole neighborhood searching for him only to discover he must have hidden in the house cleverly because he finally appeared. One snowy Sunday, as we were getting ready for church, he was running through the house. I heard him yell. My husband's suit jacket was hanging over the back of a chair still on the hanger. Somehow my son had managed to be caught by the hanger and was hanging from his eyelid. I called the family pediatricians, a wonderful couple. They quickly arranged an immediate appointment with a specialist friend of theirs. We rushed to this doctor. As I wrote this, I became aware of how personal relationships were with the doctors then. I do have wonderful doctors now, but I believe personal access was different then. My son was treated, and all is still well, hopefully. My son did have several head injuries. I used to think that he liked to back off and deliberately run into things for fun. I led a fencing club at the high school where I was teaching. Once when a babysitter was keeping the children, I received a call to go to the hospital. My son had hit his head while taking a bath. I arrived in my fencing gear, minus the mask and foil. The hospital personnel looked at me strangely and took me into a room. I realized that they were questioning me about potential child abuse. Fortunately, my son was very adept at sharing the things he would do that caused such mishaps. The babysitter verified that I wasn't even there. I thank the Lord for having his hands on my family and me.

When I was pregnant with my third child, I had some interesting situations in connection with my teaching. I will save these for a future book. A few happenings, however, I will share. One funny thing was how my chihuahua, who liked to sleep with his head on my stomach, would growl lowly when the baby would kick. Another event that might seem traumatic seemed not so much so for me by this time happened when I received a call from my daughter's school that she had broken her arm. I had my class covered and picked up my children to head to the doctor. While he was setting her arm and putting on the cast, he noticed and asked, "Are you having contractions?" I said, "I know, but I don't think I will have the baby yet." By this time, I noticed that my other two babies had been late coming, that I had good false contractions, and that I would probably have the baby suddenly on the last Monday morning of the month. On the way home, I was stopped at a red light when an ambulance rear-ended me. It was slight with no real damage. However, the emergency personnel were shocked and made certain all was well, especially because they hit a car with a very pregnant woman with two young children, one of whom had a broken arm. Surely enough, the end of the month was approaching. I went to my principal on a Friday and told him I would not be there Monday and had lesson plans ready for a week or so and would send more. I called the doctor and told him that I was going to have the baby Monday morning. He said to go to the hospital early Monday morning so he could induce labor. I was at the hospital early that Monday. My husband had gone to eat breakfast because the doctor wasn't to arrive until later. After a brief time, I called the nurse. I told her that I was having the baby. She said, "We haven't induced labor yet." I said, "I am sorry, but the baby is coming." He was. I don't believe that the doctor made it there in time. When we were bringing my new son home from the hospital, I noticed that he had a startle response when the squeaky emergency brake sounded. I remembered that in the womb, I had felt a movement similar to the way he moved. Babies must definitely hear before birth.

I do believe that the Lord truly carried me through these times as I worked and had two young children and a baby. My youngest son was about six months old when he began to become extremely ill. I walked the floor and sat up with him to help his breathing. He finally was admitted to the hospital. It was scary seeing a tiny one under oxygen. The doctor took one look at me and admitted me to the hospital. We were placed in a room together. As the children grew, of course, many events occurred that were concerning and even scary. The teen years and young adulthood for my children were filled with joys, sorrows, successes, setbacks, and heartbreaks for them as well as for me. Many a day and night, I cried unto the Lord for help, comfort, and answers. As I have learned now, I might have been more proactive with these prayers, although I did know who to run to as the situations arrived or worsened.

The arrival of grandchildren brought a new set of concerns. In some ways, these were more difficult because I was not the parent and often didn't know about the troubles until after the fact. I did start to learn more about proactive prayer. As young mothers and fathers learned about caring for little ones, sometimes panicking, I had to deal with an urge to rush in, stumbling to let them be the parent. I had one grandson who had a frightening heart issue as a baby. Another grandson miraculously was inches away from having a major artery cut as he ran through a glass door. Because my leave from work was up and I had to return home, I would have to see two small children, a newborn, and a mother crying because they were, perhaps, a little scared to be there without me. I would hear of illnesses, broken arms and legs, mishaps, accidents, and school issues. I would even see my youngest son's baby daughter ill in the hospital much as he had been, as I had seen him years earlier.

One particular pregnancy revealed to me just how powerful prayer is. The Lord taught me much during this experience. I had received terrific seats free just behind Homeplate. I was sitting at a baseball game, alone, and, frankly, feeling sorry for myself. I thought some of my children and grandchildren were coming, but no one could. I noticed a group of people behind me whose seats split the group so that they were having difficulty talking to one another. I offered them the seats I had so that they could all sit together. I just moved to an end seat by them. While sitting there, I received a message on my phone from one of my daughters-in-law, who had just been at her five-week checkup and was told the baby's heartbeat was extremely low. The doctor evidently didn't offer much hope. I must have been visibly shaken because the woman next to me asked me what was wrong. I shared with her as a few tears rolled down my cheek. I didn't share that I knew all too well how it felt to hear words about a baby's heartbeat. The group gathered around me and prayed. Then, the woman called friends and family in another state, asking them to pray. That Sunday, as I taught my third grade Sunday school class, I explained to the class how Hannah had cried and prayed for a baby. That week's story amazingly was about Samuel. I asked them if they would pray for my daughter-in-law and the baby she was carrying. I didn't share the details. They had such sweet prayers. The next week, the baby's heartbeat was fine. The pregnancy progressed well until very close to the delivery date. At her checkup, the doctor saw that the baby's heartbeat was weak. She was rushed to the hospital, and a healthy baby boy was delivered by cesarean section. I had no idea that they planned to name him Samuel. I must admit that I was taken aback by how the Lord works.

Seeing my children and grandchildren have heartbreaks, no matter how great or small, is the hardest. I know that we all must go through these, but I don't know how I would have any peace if I couldn't pray. I remember one time when one of my grandsons saw this peace. I admit that I wasn't even aware of it. We were at one of my son's house. A baby grandson was asleep in his crib. My other son's family was there as well. A tornado alert sounded. Everyone went outside to look. I stayed seated inside. The funnel was above this area. A young grandson ran back inside and asked me how I was so calm. I smiled and told him the Lord had given me peace and that all would be okay, and it was. Now, as I look back, I realize so many times that the Lord was just present, freely giving peace without my even being conscious of it.

There would be many times that I was extremely aware of the need to have rescue and peace. A few I will share now; some I will share later in this book; some I will share in a future book, the Lord willing. Twice I prayed fervently and frequently for safety, knowledge about, and peace about one who could be called my "earthquake son." He was traveling throughout Europe, backpacking after graduating from the university. I had a tentative schedule for him, showing that he should be in Athens. I admit I panicked when I heard about a major earthquake near Athens. Damage, injuries, and even many deaths were being reported. I prayed for his safety and news. I called every service I could, including the State Department, for information. I kept thinking he would find a way to contact me if he were okay. I heard no news from any source. Finally, after what seemed an unbearable time, I did receive news from him. He had changed plans and was on a remote island. He was safe, did not know about the situation, and had not been where he could keep in touch. I thanked the Lord for answering prayer and sustaining me during this time.

The next earthquake would also be a severe one. My son and his family were living in Lima, Peru. I was made aware of what they call "earthquake season" there. I heard on the news that there was a major earthquake near Lima. With each passing year, I am quicker to go to the Lord in prayer and to seek prayer from those I call my prayer warriors. I look back to other instances during my babyhood in the Lord when He just kept me safe, provided the prayer warriors, and gifted me peace.

My son was able to get word to me sooner than the other time, even though their escape was frightening. In his words, "We had a TV come sliding off a shelf only to be stopped by the cable cord, a large chandelier swinging from one side of the room to the other, the large staircase swaying, tall glass balcony doors rattling, kids, dogs, and a monkey crying and scrambling, a maid frozen in shock on the way out, and all this while trying to get down from the top floor of the apartment building." They were not able ever to return there and felt nauseated for some time afterward because of the aftershocks. Thinking about earthquakes recalls the following scripture:

> God *is* our refuge and strength, A very present help in trouble. Therefore we will not fear, Even though the earth be removed, And though the mountains be carried into the midst of the sea; *Though* its waters roar *and* be troubled, *Though* the mountains shake with its swelling. *Selah.*

Psalm 46:1–3 (NKJV)

Another Peruvian event happened when I was visiting. We rode on a train built in the late 1800s that enabled us to go high into the Andes. We were at the height of our trip when the train seemed to slip a little. The steam had to build again before we departed. I wasn't as much scared as I was awe-struck by the views we had been seeing and sick from the altitude. I did throw up a little into bags that they had available, as did one of my grandsons who was seated by me. We used the oxygen masks that helped with the altitude sickness. I was thankful when the train moved to take us to a slightly lower altitude. I learned to appreciate the tea (which didn't have a pleasant smell) that was available everywhere as we stayed high in the Andes for touring. This tea helped to alleviate the nausea. I felt the Lord in several special ways during this time. Seeing the simple life of some of those who knew how to live without modern conveniences, growing vegetables, catching fish, and raising llamas made me realize how the Lord provides. They cooked in the ground and made necessary clothing and dwellings from what was around them. Their skills showed practicality and artistry. We visited the Santa Catalina monastery, where the graphic depictions of the wounds on different life-size crucifixes prompted one of my grandsons to ask many questions about Christ and the meaning of His suffering. These discussions also had taken place when we were staying on the coast during the Easter season. I must admit that I was surprised when I watched the people gather with buckets. Something was happening in the distance. Soon fish would be coming to the shoreline. Young and old gathered the fish. They said it was about the miracle of how Jesus had provided an abundance of fish for Peter. From a rooftop there, I saw their procession of how Judas hanged himself. I held an Easter service for my family on the beach. I noticed others gathering around. After this, I again received many questions from my grandsons.

While traveling with my son, his wife, and their children in Paris, we had what was a frightful experience. We were returning from a day trip out to Versailles and were almost to our last metro stop. Cars were packed. My son and his family moved to the last car. I would need to pass a couple of cars to reach them. I motioned for him not to take that car. I couldn't be certain that he saw me, but his reactions indicated he might have made the same decision on his own. I knew that this was not a promising idea at this time because of a group of young men I saw there. One of this group grabbed my son's youngest daughter and jumped on. My son, daughter-in-law, and other two grandchildren jumped on as well. I hopped into the car in front of me, pushing to make a spot. I began praying in the Spirit. I saw people looking strangely at me when I exited the next stop. I was relieved and thankful to see all my family had exited as well. However, my son was frantically working on his phone. He had gotten my granddaughter back, fighting off the hands that were attempting to get into his pockets. In the confusion and with my son and his wife working to secure all three children, the group had managed to get his wife's billfold out of her bag. He quickly canceled or locked all accounts and cards. As soon as we returned to the apartment, he checked everything and called the police. His wife received a message that her billfold had been found. They arranged with the police to have it retrieved. Although everyone was shaken by the experience, all were fine without any monetary loss. When I say that we all were fine, I am not being as truthful as I should be. Everyone, the children, in particular, felt traumatized. I can contrast this experience with other times in Paris. In fact, I had made a trip there when this son was ten years old. My son's son, my grandson, celebrated his 10th birthday while we were in Paris. Times have changed the city, just as is the case with many large cities today. Incidents of crimes have always been with us. However, these seem to be on the increase. When one experiences an incident, especially one that threatens one's child or family, it is traumatic. I cannot imagine how a man who is a father and husband must feel when faced with such a situation. I know we were all relieved, particularly my son, when we arrived in the small, quiet towns in southern France. Encounters like this one can linger within us for years. It was not long after our return from our trip that Notre Dame burned. The sadness was intensified by the sense of loss of an era. We did have wonderful memories of enjoying Notre Dame and seeing it as it had been for centuries one last time. Maybe we felt and still do feel some anger that people and events threaten our sense of security. Thankfully, we have our Heavenly Father who is not surprised, not intimidated, and not powerless in any situation. I knew the Lord was protecting us in the moment and would continue in the process of helping us with lingering anger and the effects of trauma. The Lord is still protecting us. It has been in my later years that I began to understand more about praying in the Spirit. I knew the power of prayer and had learned how to call on my prayer warriors. My children, grandchildren, and great-grandchildren are so precious. I realize that I am helpless to deal with many of the troubles they experience, although I try. I do know how important prayer is. Several scriptures express how important it is to pray "without ceasing." I have found over the years how important this is for these loved ones. I have relied on prayer and prayer warriors for all my and my family's issues. My daughter's surgeries because of cancer caused physical and emotional stress on the entire family. My children and grandchildren have had to say goodbye to loved ones and parents. I have become keenly aware of my inability to find the words or the ways to comfort my children and grandchildren, especially with the death of a father or a husband. This feeling of helplessness brings to mind a quote from *Le Petit Prince* by Antoine de Saint-Exupéry, "*C'est un endroit tellement secret, le pays des larmes.*" The translation that captures my sentiments here is, "It is such a mysterious place, the land of tears." Estrangement from a loved one is close to this emotion. Like the Little Prince, we can just be there in silence beside the grieving person no matter what is the source of the grief. We can also pray. Despite what the world may say, prayer is powerful because it brings the Great Comforter beside us. Our loved ones also have encountered scary times, experienced separations, and dealt with day-to-day trials. Because of prayer's power and our helplessness in such situations, I encourage others to call on friends and family for prayer support. I have alerted prayer warriors to help students wake up for class, take exams, pass courses, graduate, and deal with loss, love, and hurtful friends.

Visitations and Visions

The angel of the LORD encamps all around those who fear Him, And delivers them.

Psalm 34:7 (NKJV)

Now behold, an angel of the Lord stood by him, and a light shone in the prison; and he struck Peter on the side and raised him up, saying, "Arise quickly!" And his chains fell off his hands. Then the angel said to him, "Gird yourself and tie on your sandals"; and so he did. And he said to him, "Put on your garment and follow me." So he went out and followed him, and did not know that what was done by the angel was real, but thought he was seeing a vision.

Acts 12:7–9 (NKJV)

Now the Lord spoke to Paul in the night by a vision, "Do not be afraid, but speak, and do not keep silent; for I am with you, and no one will attack you; to hurt you; for I have many people in this city."

Acts 18:9–10 (NKJV)

"Vision"

Is vision what we see,

Or really what we feel?

Sight is how we look out.

Vision is how we see in.

With what we see and

What we see within,

We can begin to live a life

With vision and wisdom.

This chapter will include aspects of some of the other chapters because these events that I call visitations and visions tend to connect to times of trouble, times of confusion, times of despair, times of drifting, in other words, times of great need. I will not share all of these. Some others may come in a future book, the Lord willing. I will begin with one that involves my mother and actually was not mine but hers. My father had passed earlier, leaving mother alone in the house. Plans were to move her to an apartment close to me to make things easier on her and easier on caring for her. I talked to her on the phone over the weekend, and she told me that she thought she saw my father in her house. Later, when I called, she did not answer. Going immediately to the house, I found her sitting on the sofa, looking very peaceful with the television still going. She had passed. This, of course, was devastating to the family and me. However, the peace I saw on her face made me think that she had had some type of visitation. I knew she had not passed alone; she had the Lord. Remembering this fact causes me to consider all those who died during COVID-19. I understand the heartbreak of their loved ones who were not able to be with those who passed alone. I hope some comfort comes with the realization of the Lord's presence at every moment, even the end, of our lives. Jesus said in Matthew 28:20 (NKJV) to those who are in Him, "…and lo, I am with you always even to the end of the age." One of my sons, when he was young, told me that he had seen Mom Casey dressed in her hat and gloves in his room saying goodbye to him just as a relative arrived to share that Mom Casey had passed. Many years later, quite recently, in fact, I have learned from two people close to me how the Lord can prepare them for their passing. My older sister, to whom I dedicated another book, told me that it was time for her to go home. I know she wanted me to be comforted. Her passing was with the Lord and peaceful. A dear friend shared with me her husband's passing and how he knew the Lord would be taking him. He prepared his wife, telling her that he would see her and their daughter in heaven. He passed peacefully in the Lord while sitting in his favorite chair.

One that I would call a visitation was when I was deeply in despair. I was in a period of drifting, confused that I had failed everyone, especially the Lord. I was caught in the mistaken idea that if I did everything I was supposed to do (works), everything would be okay. If I experienced failure or betrayal that it must be my fault. I can't say that I ever thought God was punishing me, but I felt that I must have failed. I thought I could be the

perfect woman, wife, and mother. I do remember hating
to read the scripture about the virtuous wife in Proverbs
31 (NKJV).

Who can find a virtuous wife?

For her worth is far above rubies.

The heart of her husband safely trusts her;

So he will have no lack of gain.

She does him good and not evil

All the days of her life.

She seeks wool and flax,

And willingly works with her hands.

She is like the merchant ships,

She brings her food from afar.

She also rises while it is yet night,

And provides food for her household,

And a portion for her maidservants.

She considers a field and buys it;

From her profits she plants a vineyard.

She girds herself with strength,

And strengthens her arms.

She perceives that her merchandise is good,

And her lamp does not go out by night.

She stretches out her hands to the distaff,

And her hand holds the spindle.

She extends her hand to the poor,

Yes, she reaches out her hands to the needy.

She is not afraid of snow for her household,

For all her household is clothed with scarlet.

She makes tapestry for herself;

Her clothing is fine linen and purple.

Her husband is known in the gates,

When he sits among the elders of the land.

She makes linen garments and sells them,

And supplies sashes for the merchants.

Strength and honor are her clothing;

She shall rejoice in time to come.

She opens her mouth with wisdom,

And on her tongue is the law of kindness.

She watches over the ways of her household,

And does not eat the bread of idleness.

Her children rise up and call her blessed;

Her husband also, and he praises her:

"Many daughters have done well,

But you excel them all."

Charm is deceitful and beauty is passing,

But a woman who fears the Lord, she shall be praised.

Give her of the fruit of her hands,

And let her own works praise her in the gates.

I tried in my own strength and knew that I didn't measure up to this standard. I failed to embrace the grace of the Lord as the answer and to realize that I could not control what others would do or think of me. I needed the Lord's love, mercy, and help. I have learned that hurts by others can chip away at a person. Although I had felt that I had not been affected, each small one and each attempt in my own strength left me more vulnerable to drift away from seeking the Lord's help. Betrayals further weakened me. Once I reached a point where I felt I might take my life. The Lord had not left me. He loves me. I felt a strong hand gripping my shoulder. I looked. No person was there. I intuitively knew that it was the Lord. I knew He was with me. I knew that I would not follow such a course. Times would still bring more troubles. I would sometimes drift back into my feelings that although I knew that the Lord would not stop loving me or ever leave me, I would try to hide from him. Perhaps, this is similar to how Adam and Eve felt when they disobeyed. Perhaps, it was like I felt as a little girl when I asked mother to spank me but not to ask why. I would sometimes still feel like that though I knew that I was saved and that the Lord loved me and that I was not pleasing Him. It was during this period that I wrote the following.

"Failing, Falling"

Responsibility is the control, the key,

That keeps all things in balance, guarding my destiny.

Feeling the stress, the fatigue, the constant pressure,

Not to falter, to fail keeping to the measure.

Then, because of a human frailty, a single flaw,

And the world instantly seems to crumble, even fall.

And because of a single moment lost in time,

I didn't remember; I didn't toe the line.

The Lord has shown such patience with me as He has helped me peel away those confusing ideas from religion versus the relationship that He wanted to have with me.

Another time was when I was scared. I mentioned earlier that I have myasthenia gravis. I discovered I had this disease thanks to my family doctor, who went to my church, and the wonderful neurologist I still have. I had been dropping things. I had very few glasses left in the house. My family physician looked at my hands and thought something was wrong. He arranged an appointment with a neurologist. What concerned him about the look of my hands was not the issue. The neurologist diagnosed me with MG, or as was known then as "the disease nobody knows." At that time, there weren't very many options. I remember hearing that only 15% lived with it. I would weaken, even to the point that I might not be able to open my eyes, move, talk, or swallow very well. I awoke one night particularly afraid. I couldn't call out or move. Inside I could ask the Lord for help. A bright light appeared and moved close to me. I felt love, peace, and lessening of my symptoms. One additional experience with this during the onset of my diagnosis involved a picture my students took of me while I was still struggling. My principal bought a comfortable tall chair and podium for me so I could sit to teach and prop myself up with my hands and arms using the podium. Polaroid cameras that instantly printed were popular at that time. One of my students took a picture of me. The class went into shock as they saw what looked like transparent arms on either side of me. I believe that I was literally being lifted up. I loved teaching, and we needed my income; however, I thought I couldn't continue teaching because I wasn't able to teach the way I used to do. I had a wonderful district consultant who had gone to my old high school. She took me to see a teacher who was in a wheelchair. She let me know that it was my mind and heart that were necessary and not my legs and arms. I would eventually realize that, as written in Romans 11:18 (NKJV), "But if you do boast, *remember that* you do not *support* the root, but that the root supports you." Over the years, many changes and events occurred that have allowed me to lead a pretty normal life. I would later find help through diet and medicine developed through the help of the Jerry Lewis Telethons. Yes, I was and am one of Jerry's kids. Most importantly, I am a child of the Lord (the root), who would remind me that "Those who wait on the LORD shall renew *their* strength; they shall mount up with wings like eagles, they shall run and not be weary, they shall walk and not faint" (Isaiah 40:31, KJV).

I mentioned earlier how tired I was working and caring for three children. One time, I was so exhausted that I just cried and told the Lord, "I can't do this!" The doorbell rang. I opened the door. Two young men were there who called me by my first name. They talked to me, and I was comforted, and my strength and spirit renewed. I closed the door. Then, it hit me. Who were they? How did they know my name? Immediately, I opened the door and stepped outside. I looked up and down the street. They were not to be found. I had not seen or heard a vehicle. It had been less than a minute since I closed the door. The only conclusion was that they were heavenly messengers sent to aid me. One reason that I say this is that feeling of being helped by such a messenger has occurred two other times. Each of these times, I have been protected or comforted, and yet I didn't seem to wonder about them until just afterward. It is an indescribable sensation. Another example was when I was returning from a workshop I presented. I had a layover and was waiting for my plane. I went into one of the shops to buy a snack. A large, angry man was at the checkout counter. I suddenly was frozen, thinking he was going to harm someone. I saw a person move toward him and place a hand on him. The ill-tempted man immediately calmed down. However, he didn't seem to acknowledge the person or the touch. The store attendant didn't acknowledge the person either. The person looked briefly at me but said nothing. I was on the plane talking to a young woman who was on her way to her first job as an ophthalmologist. I glanced back and noticed that same person sitting a few seats back, looking at me. I noticed that the flight attendant did not seem to acknowledge that person. After I debarked from the plane, I looked and did not see that person come off the plane. I say "a person" because I remember thinking is that a man or a woman. I couldn't tell by clothes, hair, or physical appearance. The person was pleasant and peaceful looking. Now, I had that same feeling I had with the door experience. A third experience was when I was concerned about my daughter and the arrival of a new baby. I was with students at an away competition. I arose early and went to an inside courtyard to talk to the Lord and have my coffee. A woman, whom I thought worked there, came over to me and asked why I was troubled. I shared. I don't know why, but I poured out my heart and concerns to a total stranger. She spoke to me as though she knew me. Again, I felt that strange sensation and was left with comfort and strength. She walked away. I looked up, and she was nowhere to be found. I cannot say with certainty; only the Lord knows. However, these visitations were unique and had someone definitely doing the Lord's work.

Much more numerous and I am learning to believe, just as important are the many times that the Lord permits me to see His presence helping, guiding, and protecting me. I know that I realized His presence when I was young. As I grew older, He was still there. However, I can look back and see how I blocked my realization because I began to rely on myself more than Him. Like a stubborn little spiritual toddler, I would say, "No," not totally understanding what I was doing. Actually, I became a little more like the toddler who says, "I do myself." Sometimes this was out of fear; sometimes, out of confusion; sometimes, out of misplaced confidence; sometimes, perhaps, even out of rebellion. Then, I became a spiritual adolescent who didn't want to be disobedient, but I thought, *Okay, Lord, I know what I should do. I have got this!* How many mistakes I made and how many disappointments I experienced because of this mistaken idea that my understanding and strength were not His. As I saw myself spiritually as an adult, I thought, *Lord, what's wrong with me? I shouldn't be having this much trouble.* These were mistaken views. I am learning that true special growth means learning that I can do nothing without the Lord. As the song says, "I need thee every hour most gracious Lord" (*I Need Thee Every Hour*, Annie Hawks, 1872). As I learn to seek Him, I find Him. There is nothing too great or nothing too small for discussion. Am I consistent in doing this? Unfortunately, I am not, but I am faster to realize and return to the seeking. He comes in small ways and often uses others to let me see His presence.

I have shared in this book how the police came to my rescue. I shared in a previous book a special Christmas incident. Another came unexpectedly late one wintry night as I was coming home from a work-related meeting in a nearby town. I heard a noise; my car swerved; I had a flat. I got out of the car and began trying to figure out how to change the tire. I was tired, and the cold wasn't helping. This was prior to cellphones, so I had no other option. A tall truck pulled over at a short distance behind me. I can still see the word *fish* as it was written on the side of the truck. A tall, strong-looking young man looked at my dilemma and quietly offered to help. I must admit that I was a little scared, although I tried to appear strong. He changed the tire and refused to take the little money that I offered him. I said, "Thank you." He went back to his truck, and we both drove away. I thanked the Lord. A similar, although perhaps even more life-threatening, incident occurred years later. I knew immediately to call upon the Lord by this time rather than offer the thank you after the fact. At this time, I was living in the Texas Panhandle. It was late September; I was returning from work I had to do in Houston. When I arrived at the airport, it was snowing. I had not prepared all the necessary supplies in my car that I normally would have for winter weather there because it seemed a little early for snow. I learned that September is not too early, and April is not too late. I called my husband to see how it was where we lived. We lived in a nearby town. Unfortunately, this was a time when I was not staying proactive in asking for the Lord's guidance. The fact that my car didn't have blankets, food, and water was one proof. The fact that I didn't pray about driving on a rather lonely road during a snowstorm to where I lived testifies to my failure to seek His guidance. I should never have left. As I drove, the wind howled, and the snow was blowing horizontally. This was a blizzard! My car was finally blown off the road into a field. I tried to get the car back on the road but was unable to do so. My cellphone didn't work (we had such devices by then). This was not unusual at spots on this road, even in clear weather. I was dressed in short sleeves and had no wrap because it had been very warm in Houston. Nothing in my suitcase would even help. At this point, I did start praying. I had a moment of hope and then increased despair when I saw a police car speed past. I waited, hoping it would return. I thought, *I could freeze to death!* Evidently, no one can even see me. My car would run out of gas. Night would come, meaning no hope of cars and an even colder temperature. My conversation with the Lord became much more personal as I realized I was in His hands. I was thankful that I knew I was not alone. As I was in prayer, I heard a tap on the window. I saw a large man in attire one would expect for the Texas Panhandle in a blizzard. He was a rancher. He used his heavy truck to pull me onto the road. He told me in a strong voice, "Lady, I better drive your car. You ride with my wife in the truck. She'll drive." They drove me all the way to my house and continued with where they were going. I do regret that I didn't get their name or contact information. I would have liked to do something for them. However, that is the way of especially the ranchers and many others in the Texas Panhandle. They just take care of people and the livestock. They don't expect anything from it. The Lord wasn't ready to take me home yet, but He was proving to me that He was there and that He uses people to do His work.

He would lead me into deep relationships that would help to guide me and give me comfort. After a major move, I felt lonely and went through some trying times. It was my birthday; however, this might be an uneventful one. I gathered some comfort from the fact that this particular year my birthday fell on the same day as the National Day of Prayer. Having been searching for a new church home, I headed to a small church I had seen that was near to my house. When I arrived, I didn't see any cars. A person appeared and asked if he could help me. I explained that I was new in the area and was hoping to be with others for the National Day of Prayer. He explained that this congregation was gathering at a larger church. He offered to unlock the sanctuary so I could go in there to pray. I entered, went to the altar at the front, and, alone in the sanctuary, unloaded my fears, concerns, and heartbreaks to the Lord. I felt a warmth on my face and looked up. The sun was shining through the stained-glass window. I smiled, almost laughing as I said, "Oh, thank you, Lord, for my birthday present." Unlike any I had seen before, the stained-glass window had a beautiful butterfly in its center. I have always loved butterflies and what they symbolize to me. I don't believe there is a room in my house without butterflies. This love for butterflies must have been apparent even when my children were young. My daughter, when she was just learning to write sentences in school, printed a short poem to give to me:

Butterfly hover near my mother,

And tell her that I dearly love her.

Not long ago, she framed the faded little note along with a newly printed one of that poem. How beautiful are the inspirations and faith of a child! Adults do need to value these in children and look back to their own childhood to search for reflections of such faith! One of the paintings I have done that I consider my only decent work is a butterfly. I knew then and even more so now that we are in Christ being transformed day by day, though painful at times, into the beautiful state when we will be with Him forevermore. I knew that I was to attend this church. The story connected with this church and its people has more to tell. One day when I was feeling a little down and even fearful, I went walking at a trail near my house. I met a lovely lady with whom I felt an immediate connection. I shared my heart and concerns. It happened that she attended that church, and her husband was the leader of one of the studies I was to take. I became friends with the entire family, and friendship continues. They are my go-to prayer warriors, along with other dear friends in Christ I would meet there. I do believe that the Lord can guide us to each other when we are open to Him. I see this in scripture in too many places to list here. I have experienced myself, especially in later years, His direction. Once I felt led to send a check and a letter to a man, who at that time I barely knew from doing some repair work for me. I was to tell him that the Lord recognized his service. Another time, I received a small bonus from a person whose son I helped. With the envelope in my pocket, I then met a woman and was led to give it to her. I discovered she had a medical bill to pay. I sometimes awaken in the middle of the night with an urging to pray for someone or something, only later to discover why. One time before I had really begun to understand better these promptings, I had a dream of snow and sounds of distress. I heard things in my dream but couldn't see as much as in my other dreams. I heard children crying. I prayed with tears and a broken heart for these children. The next day, I learned a roof had collapsed from heavy snow accumulation, killing parents at a celebration. Their children were not with them. Another time, I awoke sensing a need to pray for a particular person. I received a call not long afterward that a loved one had passed. I have received emails, calls, and special needs met that can only be explained by the Lord's prompting, especially because some of these came from people I don't personally know. I have asked questions and/or help from the Lord in prayer and had daily devotionals, songs, programs, or other events to answer questions and meet needs. I had a beautiful musical dream one night that I am still trying to understand. I heard dueling pianos playing a heavenly tune. I searched for several days online, trying to find the tune. I believe that I have found it. However, I heard arrangements in my dream that go well beyond anything I can find played or on sheet music. I have given the sheet music to one of my grandsons for him to play and tried to explain the marvelous enhancements that I heard. This "musical dream" gave me these two lines and continues to remind me of my Lord, His glory, and His love:

Power, Protection, and Peace the Spirit brings.

Juried, Justified, Joyed my soul sings!

As I share some of my experiences, I wonder how could so many of these happenings, when preprogrammed, prewritten, or predetermined in time, just happen to come at the appropriate moment for my need unless guided by the Lord. How can I account for my being led or just happening to be there when I altered my actions or movements because of prompting to become a part of an answer or deliver help if it were not for the Lord? How can I account for things that have no good explanation but were physically felt and seen in connection with my immediate need and/or prayer if it is not the Lord? I have written about only some of these events. There are many more. I am learning to grow in my relationship with the Lord so that I might understand who He is. I am beginning to understand better what Paul was praying for in these verses:

> I have never stopped thanking God for you. I pray for you constantly, asking God, the glorious Father of our Lord Jesus Christ, to give you wisdom to see clearly and really understand who Christ is and all that he has done for you. I pray that your hearts will be flooded with light so that you can see something of the future He has called you to share. I want you to realize that God has been made rich because we who are Christ's have been given to Him! I pray that you will begin to understand how incredibly great His power is to help those who believe Him. It is that same mighty power.
>
> **Ephesians 1:16–19 (TLB)**

"The Beauty of Redemption"

The soft, white lily's swaying in the breeze

Thoughts echo out in gentle, sweet purity.

But faintly in the midst, I begin to see,

Images of a face wrecked in agony.

The visage wears a crown stained in blood and tears.

The patient look accepts with calm the pain and shame.

Only a word would end it all, but silently He bears.

Oh! Loving me, He for my sins endures the blame.

My heart is torn but uplifted in the view.

I want the vision, but I turn—the irony.

I see the understanding eyes, He knew

I would fall but follow one day again faithfully.

As fast as it did come, the sight began to fade.

The ivory flower, chaste and pure, was all that remained.

From grotesque wrong, beauty He had made.

So with His love and sacrifice, I am redeemed—saved.

Epilogue

Where can I go from Your Spirit? Or where can
I flee from Your Presence?

Psalm 139:7 (NKJV)

"Knowing I Am in Your Presence"

In Your Presence, I'm meant to be.

Safe, secure my soul You set free.

So why do I wander, even hide?

Lost, alone, not letting Your Spirit Guide?

Your loving chord with patient voice,

Gentle, sweet call leaves it my choice.

Now I run to Your loving arm,

Rescued, safe as You guard from harm.

For some strange reason, I had my outline before I formally began to write. Oh, I had some parts written down, some drafted in my mind, some developing within my heart, and the poems, most hidden in an old brief-case. I was led to add an epilogue, although I admit that I have no idea why. I don't believe I have ever written one or have ever sensed a need for one. Now, I know why. This writing process became more than sharing. It has been and is the Lord refining and guiding me into new insight. Even today and probably until the last edit, I will be gaining in new insights and understanding about my journey, His word, and my purposes. I will try to provide many of these insights ranging from each section beginning with "A Mother's Prayer."

Mothers, grandmothers, great-grandmothers, and those who feel or serve as such have immeasurable opportunities to guide children from before birth and throughout the children's lives. Prayer and growing in relationship with the Lord are the keys for these guides. Some of these precious guides have shared that they, too, had visions and heard words from the Lord. Most often, these are words and sights connected to prayers for safety or healing of children and grandchildren. One hears, "Your child will be okay. You can cease your worries and prayers." One sees a light similar to one I saw.

This light brings comfort and even renewed strength. Many do not share these sights and sounds with anyone. Concerns for what others might think or say about us stop many. The reasons can vary and be personal. I understand because these are very intimate moments with the Lord. I really didn't want to share many of these in writing. Some I share here I have never shared before. I thought by this point in my writing I would know why I was told to do so. Maybe, I am sharing this for those who need to know others have had such experiences. Maybe, I am to overcome the fear that others will think that I am strange. However, even with failures and late starts with this process, they, as well as I, can begin anew each day so that those dearly loved ones can be protected by and drawn to the Lord. Even young children can know the Lord and feel His presence. We should never dissuade or fail to see that they can. Child-like faith is a blessing. The child needs to be helped to develop a personal relationship with the Lord. Dos and don'ts should be coupled with explanations as possible and should not displace the importance of relationship with the Lord and seeking His help. Memorizing scripture to put the message into the heart can be of immense help to the child now and in the future. I can share that one recent time when I had a head injury that having scripture in my heart was profitable and powerful, especially when I heard the neurosurgeon say that the brain bleed was too deep for operation. A future MRI revealed no bleeding. Praise the Lord! This injury and recuperation period combined several of the things that the Lord had shown me about being in His presence and under His wings. Prior to my waking up ill and hurting my head, one of my grandsons had already planned to move in with me temporarily as he transitioned to a new job from one in another city. Another grandson was also to be near me for a short time. I needed some extra care during my recuperation. One grandson would "Granny sit" and take me to the doctor. They both had a joke about driving Miss Granny. The one who would stay with me would help with cooking, among other things. The pandemic hit shortly after this event. Because of my myasthenia gravis, the doctor advised me to avoid contact with others. My injury had isolated me even before the major outbreak, providing an early protection hedge. Isolation was an issue for me and many others. Having at least one grandson in the house gave me some additional company as his job had him working remotely. Were all these things just coincidences? I think not. Waking at night, sometimes afraid, led me to learn new scriptures by heart. Proverbs 3:24 (NKJV) says, "When you lie down, you will not be afraid; Yes, you will lie down and your sleep will be sweet." I was able to return to sweet sleep. I became keenly aware of just how much I needed the Lord and how He was with me.

His Word, coupled with prayer, is important at every point. Children and adults need to know that they should pray about everything and not worry about anything. Nothing is too small or too big for the Lord to handle. We must be careful with children, adults, and ourselves to avoid trying to grow in the Lord without His help and guidance. When doubts and questions arise, the Lord has the answers, and we should not be afraid to ask. We need to help children, adults, and ourselves understand that we are now under grace and not under the law. Denominations and religion can confuse and steer all astray if the focus is not on the completed work of Jesus Christ to cover the cost of our sins and that the believer must accept His free gift of grace. Often, denominations have this core but become locked into a small compartment of what all this means and what can result.

When Christ died on the cross, paying the ultimate price for us, the veil in the temple was ripped supernaturally from top to bottom, establishing with the following burial and resurrection the new covenant as prophesied in the Old Testament. We see in 2 Corinthians 3 (NKJV) the limitations yet power of this new covenant over the old covenant, "Not that we are sufficient of ourselves to think of anything as being from ourselves, but our sufficiency is from God, who also made us sufficient as ministers of the new covenant, not of the letter but of the Spirit; for the letter kills, but the Spirit gives life." We now have the personalized connection through the indwelling of the Holy Spirit when we accept the grace gift but then still have free choice as to how we access all that this means. Some keep trying to go back to the law, establishing a works-based way of covering sin. I can understand this prideful tendency to think that we need to do something. In fact, we do need to believe, accept, and follow. However, the work is to allow the Holy Spirit to guide, teach, and mentor us even in this process. We are to grow in relationship, not religious practices. Special ways or rituals (practices) that we do are wonderful if they move us to, remind us of, and connect us with the Lord both collectively and, most importantly, personally. God did not send His son for us to be condemned but to be saved. We can stifle our growth in relationships through feelings of shame and condemnation. I would encourage the reader to read John 17 prayerfully and slowly. It reveals so much of the heart of

God the Father and of His son. We are able to hear Jesus' prayer for his disciples and for us—such love. We can see God's plan as it had been from the beginning, was then, and is now. God's sending His son, Christ's sacrifice, and the Holy Spirit's dwelling are because of love. These truths are so overwhelming that we have trouble imagining it completely. When I realized the true meaning of "the greatest of these is love" in the gifting of the Spirit and my inability to love as the Lord loves, I began my journey back from the law, from trying to do everything myself to His love and grace. I could see that He never left me and that I just needed to let Him in. He was saying, "Behold, I stand at the door and knock. If anyone hears My voice and opens the door, I will come in to him and dine with him, and him with Me" (Revelation 3:20, NKJV). When we begin that very personal, one-on-one relationship with the Lord, we begin to see who He is and His love. It reminds me of the song lyrics, "Turn your eyes upon Jesus. Look full in His wonderful face, and the things of earth will grow strangely dim, in the light of His glory and grace" (The Heavenly Vision, Helen Howarth Lemme, 1918). As a child, I think that I did this more, crawling up into a loving parent's lap, talking about everything, and asking all those wonderful questions. I stayed near to Him in simple trust and faith. Just as then, now I say, "Yes, Jesus loves me; this I know for the Bible tells me so." ("Say and Seal," originally poem by Anna Bartlett Warner, 1860). As a broken adult, I felt His hand on my shoulder. As a prodigal daughter, I felt Him joyously embracing me, welcoming me back home. As an imperfect heir to His family, He helped and continues to help me to understand His presence and how the Holy Spirit works in me, mentors, protects, corrects, and teaches me. I could then and now begin to see more clearly the truth revealed in His Word and work. I could see how I often closed and opened the door to direct communication, fellowship, and communion to have heaven here on earth.

As I learn to keep this door wide open, I see and understand more. I marvel at how scriptures I have read hundreds of times burst forth with new and greater meaning. I can begin each morning anticipating what the Lord has in store. I can more easily give my failures, needs, worries, and questions to Him throughout the day. I can talk to Him at night in my bed about where I missed and where correction is needed. I can pray for others, their needs, and their salvation. Sometimes when I am really tired, I may fall asleep praying. Sometimes I awake in the middle of the night to finish prayers or feel a special need to pray for someone. Sometimes, I am so tired that I ask the Holy Spirit to pray for me. I try not to linger in regret such that I keep this door open more often and wider than in the past. I will admit sometimes I do, and sometimes the door still may swing to just a crack now, but I don't let it shut and am quicker throwing it open wide again. I am so glad that I have learned more about my armor so that I realize that I don't have to feel vulnerable and that just as Christ told us, He has conquered the world, sin, and death and that I am safe under His wings.

Although I have always liked reading the Bible and saw it as God's word, each day, I am increasingly amazed and drawn to it. I know there were times when I held passages close for instruction, truth, guidance, comfort, and security. However, parts, I believe I might have studied academically. I do believe I learned much, even from this. Now, it is through single words, phrases, verses, passages, and connections throughout the Bible that are lighting up exponentially, almost more than I can fathom. I find it hard even to describe. Looking to the original Hebrew and Greek, although I am a beginner, only expands this process. I will write more about this in a future book, the Lord willing. I can see the continuity of single authorship in the Bible though written by different human writers with unique styles over the centuries. I know that the Spirit is enabling this insight and not any ability of my own. He even is the one driving my hunger for more. I just need to keep the door open and ask. I have failed to mention one way I see to keep the door open. It is praise and thankfulness. I found a quote by C. S. Lewis that may explain what I am seeing, "It is in the process of being worshipped that God communicates His presence to men." I have read in scripture much about worship. I knew that when I talked to God, trying in simple faith to trust and obey Him, I felt more in His presence. Was this worship? Was I to fall on my face to worship? Was I to sing songs of praise? Was I to do all the things that I seemed to see mentioned in scripture? I looked to John 4:24 (NKJV), "God is Spirit, and those who worship Him must worship in spirit and truth." I searched in Matthew 4:10 (NKJV), "Then Jesus said to him, 'Away with you, Satan! For it is written, You shall worship the Lord your God, and Him only you shall serve.' Then those who were in the boat came and worshiped Him [Jesus], saying, 'Truly You are the Son of God.'" (Matthew 14:33, NKJV) I begin to see more than a position of worship, more than a sound of worship, and even more than a service of worship. I saw the Trinity—God the Father, the Son, and the Holy Spirit. I saw God's plan and way to bring us into a relationship, personal and familial. I don't think this understanding diminishes in any way the other ways or the awe and reference in worship. It magnifies it. The Hebrew helped me develop more perspective. I do encourage the reader to learn more about the names of God. However, I found the use of Elohim, as used in Genesis 1:1, showed me that the God Head is three in one, operating singularly but separately at the same time. The Hebrew word is plural yet acts structurally in the verse as one in concert—just a little confusing. I apologize if I am inapt or astray in explanation, but this is how I am seeing it. The Hebrew for worship is Shachah, but it is spelled with Hebrew letters that are shin chet hey. I searched, looking at the early letter symbols to try to understand both what it was as a picture of as well as all the meanings. A man holding up his arms and hands while standing is the picture for hey. It seems that it can have a range of meanings breath, sigh, look, and, interestingly, behold or reveal, especially in reference to a great site. I had a little difficulty with chet because I found the modern symbol was connected to the ancient Hhet; finding the sound for the double h is ch sound. The original symbol evidently was of a wall for a tent and denoted protection from the outside. In my opinion, I can see this as protection both physically and spiritually. Teeth was the picture symbol originally for shin. Its meaning was not only teeth but also chewing, consuming, pressing, or destroying. I found many variations of this symbol. I must mention that there are additional meanings and significances of the numbers that these represent, such as mystical meanings. Although, as a small child, I saw special significance to certain numbers between one and ten, I don't want the reader to think that I spend my time researching every word and number. I only explore when I feel led to do so. I am noticing that usually, these few times are to help me see something better that I need to know at a particular time. Leaving these for future understanding, I considered just the basics I could see so far. I could see three in the teeth, although I read something about two. God is three in one to me. There is all power and might in the Godhead, but there is also consuming or taking in and pressing into the shape desired (work of the Holy Spirit?). I know that worship does include the understanding of the truth of God's position above all. I discovered that this symbol also signifies the number 300, which can mean the perfect lamb sacrifice that stands for the final, perfect blood sacrifice of Christ. Could part of worship be understanding and being in awe of these truths? Could worship also entail the drawing into the protective wall, the sanctuary, the secret place of the most high? Could worship be grounded in these first points but initiate as we look upward, breathing in and beholding His majesty, sighing in the realization of our inabilities and humble position, yet seeing His revelations of what He has done, what He is doing, what He plans to do, and how much He loves us? Again, a quote by C. S. Lewis suggests a point about being in a state of worship that draws us into His presence: "The real test of being in the presence of God is that you either forget about yourself altogether or see yourself as a small, dirty object" (Mere Christianity). The law of the Old Testament does show us that we are "dirty" but that a Holy, Merciful God knows we cannot cleanse ourselves. The grace of the New Testament shows us not only the Lord's sacrificial plan to cleanse us but also how His love can engulf us so that we can forget about ourselves and dwell in His love and peace. His love is helping me to completely forget about myself. I am in process, much as depicted in the song, So Long Self (MercyMe, 2006). I am definitely not a scholar in any of these matters. I am an imperfect Christ follower who is just trying to show the reader some of the ways He has saved me, been with me, helped me, shown me, and loved me. I am trying to explain what I am incapable of doing—what it means to me to be in His presence and under His wings.

Great Christmas Gift!

You might also like a lovely Christmas gift that has paintings and greeting card verses as well as personal memories of past and present Christmas celebrations. Designed as a small but meaningful gift.

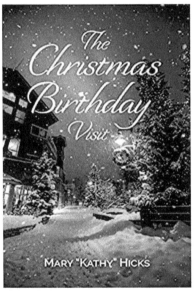

Available online at Trilogy Book Store, Amazon, Barnes and Nobles, Half Price Bookstore, and many other sites.

Author's website:marykathyhicks.com

Reviews Amazon:

Sporter

5.0 out of 5 stars **GOD's greatest gift…his son CHRIST JESUS!**

Awesome story and a beautiful reminder to me of my own past Christmas. The joy, the Holy Spirit, and the disappointments. Most of all, a reminder of the true spirit of Christmas. The gift of Christ Jesus! Highly recommended!!!

Frances Woolf

5.0 out of 5 stars **It sums up the mystery of the story.**

This is a book of Christmas wonder and nostalgia through the eyes of the author. It so vividly depicts the joys and traditions of Christmas. A very enjoyable story that I highly recommend.

Christine Walton

5.0 out of 5 stars. **Heartfelt and Spirit-filled**

Heartfelt and personal story told by the author. You can tell she has a strong connection to the Holy Spirit.

SARAH

5.0 out of 5 stars **The real reason for Christmas**

The author did a remarkable job at taking the reader down memory lane of Christmas traditions while focusing on the true meaning. The book was a joy to read and would bless all who read it. Highly recommend.

5.0 out of 5 stars **Outstanding!! Great and inspiring story of the true meaning of Christmas!!**

This story and account of Christmas and how it has changed over the years is a must-read for all ages. This is an incredible and moving explanation of what Christmas should be about, and the author creates a context to feel its true meaning.

Barnes and Nobles Reviews:

Jobuse, TX

5 out of 5 stars

Excellent Read!! This was a perfect book to read for the holidays! It is a special time of year, and this book captures that feeling very well! Tags: Life Changing, Inspirational, Emotional, Quick Read, Couldn't Put It Down

Loved by God, Bedford, TX

5 out of 5 stars

Perfect! This was a wonderful uplifting book. Very enjoyable, and I highly recommend it. I could connect to her feelings of nostalgia and the joys of Christmas. The book brought our focus on the wonders of Christmas.

✔ Yes, I recommend